THE OTHER ISRAEL

Voices of Refusal and Dissent

◆

FOREWORD BY TOM SEGEV
INTRODUCTION BY ANTHONY LEWIS

Edited by Roane Carey and Jonathan Shainin

THE NEW PRESS

NEW YORK
LONDON

Requests for permission to reproduce selections from this book should be
made through our website: https://thenewpress.com/contact.

Published in the United States by The New Press, New York, 2002
Distributed by Two Rivers Distribution

An earlier version of Chapter 3 appeared in the Fall 2000 issue of
Middle East Report
Chapters 5 and 7 © 2002 *The Guardian*
An abridged version of Chapter 6 appeared in *Between the Lines*
Chapters 9, 14, 23, 26, 28, 30, 33, and 36 © 2001 and 2002 *Ha'aretz*
Chapter 12 originally appeared in *The Progressive*
Chapter 17 © 2002 *The New York Times*
All other essays © by each author.

All royalties from this book will be donated to
Israeli human rights and peace organizations.

ISBN 978-1–56584–873–3 (hc)
ISBN 978-1–56584–940–2 (pb)
CIP data available

The New Press publishes books that promote and enrich public discussion
and understanding of the issues vital to our democracy and to a more
equitable world. These books are made possible by the enthusiasm of our
readers; the support of a committed group of donors, large and small; the
collaboration of our many partners in the independent media and the not-
for-profit sector; booksellers, who often hand-sell New Press books;
librarians; and above all by our authors.

www.thenewpress.com

Composition by dix!

Printed in the United States of America

CONTENTS

EDITORS' NOTE

Roane Carey and Jonathan Shainin

IT IS A COMMON enough characteristic of the American media that it will reach for the easy cliché or the crude simplification. This is perhaps more true with respect to foreign affairs, given the minimal time and space allowed such matters by our entertainment-besotted culture. Ever heedful of the bottom line and the presumed low attention span of the consumer, our information merchants recoil from complexity.

It should therefore come as no surprise that the Middle East conflict is generally explained here as a struggle between merely two sides, Israelis and Palestinians; even worse, it's often characterized as a battle between Ariel Sharon and Yasser Arafat, as if geopolitics and a century of conflict could be reduced to a boxing match. "Support for Israel" is thus automatically interpreted to mean uncritical endorsement of the repressive measures used to enforce Israel's occupation of the West Bank and Gaza Strip.

In fact, a significant number of Israelis have challenged Sharon's policies, and they have done so out of a deep love and concern for their country. As former Knesset member Shulamit Aloni writes in this volume, "Whoever claims that the settlements are Israel's catastrophe from a security and an economic point of view is not an anti-Semite but a patriot. Whoever condemns the demolition of houses and opposes the provocative liquidations does so out of love for their homeland." Those Israelis who are speaking out against the occupation realize that it facilitates the most regressive tendencies within Israel: It encourages extremist elements in the settler movement and the ultra-Orthodox community; it threatens the recent and tenuous gains of the "constitutional revolution," which has strengthened civil liberties; and it endangers the fragile rights of the country's one million Palestinian citizens, who are now being branded as a dangerous "fifth column."

These dissenting voices—too often overlooked by international observers—are numerous and diverse. This book, owing to limitations of time and space, showcases only a portion of the vital work done by many individuals and by groups like New Profile, Ta'ayush, Women in Black, B'Tselem, the Public Committee Against Torture in Israel, Machsom Watch, Adalah, Rabbis for Human Rights, and others.

Consider *The Other Israel*, then, to be an act of solidarity and recognition: solidarity with those Israelis who are brave enough to risk the ostracism of their countrymen in speaking out for justice and human rights; and recognition of their contribution to the cause of decency and a just solution to the conflict.

UNE 2002

FOREWORD

Tom Segev

GABRIEL STERN, ONE of the more decent—though lesser known—journalists in the history of Israeli journalism, once told me of a traumatic but formative experience that occurred during his military service. He was thirty-five at the time, having come to Israel from Germany a decade previously. He had studied Middle Eastern Studies at Hebrew University and participated in Judah Leib Magnes's and Martin Buber's peace activism. Stern was not a pacifist, but he was extremely fearful of any form of violence. In 1948, during Israel's War of Independence, he was drafted and posted on guard duty at the Italian Hospital, located in close proximity to what would later become the line dividing Israeli West Jerusalem and the eastern, Arab part of the city. As he wandered aimlessly around the deserted hospital one day, he suddenly came face to face with a uniformed man armed with a rifle. The man was standing at the end of a long, dim corridor. Stern did not know how the man had got there, but he sensed his life was in danger: One of the two was bound to open fire. Stern looked the man in the eyes; the man looked back at him. Stern raised his rifle; the man raised his, finger on the trigger. It was clear to Stern that he who shot first would live. The other would die. He pulled the trigger. The bullet penetrated the figure standing in front of him and shattered it into a thousand fragments of

Translated by Jessica Cohen

glass. It was a large mirror. Stern had shot at himself. He never fired a gun again.

Stern was a family friend, and I knew him as a child. At the age of about six, I once asked him what a border was. His reply was to take me on a field trip along the barbed-wire fences, the landmine fields and the row of boarded-up houses that divided Jerusalem. We could see a Jordanian soldier on the Old City walls in the distance, armed with a rifle and binoculars. He observed us as we watched him. "No," said Gabriel, "a border is not the line that separates the good guys from the bad guys. There are good guys on the other side of the border too, but they don't know there are good guys on our side, and that is why there is war."

Gabriel Stern was one of the good guys on our side. It is no surprise that I recall him now, as I begin to write a foreword to a collection of essays, all of which sound voices of dissent. Until his death in 1983, Stern worked at the small leftist daily newspaper *Al Hamishmar* ("On Guard"), the organ of the United Workers Party, Mapam, most of whose supporters were members of Hashomer Hatzair kibbutzim. Stern believed in human kindness and, consequently, he also believed in peace. In his gentle way, he fought fiercely against any manifestation of discrimination in Israeli society, whether directed toward Jews or Arabs. He believed in peace between the State of Israel and its neighbors. After the Six-Day War, he renewed his faith in the dream of creating a binational existence in the Land of Israel, based on equality and mutual respect.

I take this opportunity to commemorate Stern not only because my attempts to have a street named after him have thus far failed, but also because his voice was not a solitary one: Similar voices often figured in Israeli public discourse and were also prominent in the Hebrew press. The central point that readers of this collection should recognize is that its contributors are bolstered by a long tradition: Voices of dissent and Jewish humanism have accompanied the Zionist movement since its inception.

Prominent Zionist essayist Ahad Ha'Am published his travel impressions in an 1891 article entitled "Truth from the Land of Israel." Among other things, it included his observation that Jewish pioneering settlers "treat the Arabs with hostility and cruelty, trespass unjustly on their territories, beat them shamelessly for no sufficient reason, and boast at having done so." He attributed the phenomenon to a psychological cause: "They were slaves in their land of exile and suddenly they find they have unlimited freedom, wild freedom.... This sudden change has produced in their hearts an inclination toward repressive despotism, as always occurs when 'the slave becomes king.' " Ahad Ha'Am warned: "Overseas, we are accustomed to thinking of the Arabs as desert savages, as a donkey-like people that neither sees nor comprehends what is going on around it. But . . . if a time should come when the life of our people in the Land of Israel develops until it encroaches upon the natives to a smaller or greater extent, they will not easily yield their position. . . ."

Other writers also sought ways to solve "the Arab problem," as it was termed in the early days of Zionism. The Zionist movement was never content to have fulfilled its dream forcibly, and continuously attempted to convince itself that it was also fulfilling it rightfully. The need to be counted not only among the powerful, but also among the just, caused David Ben-Gurion, for example, to invest many hours in conversation with J. L. Magnes, head of Hebrew University in the 1940s; philosopher Martin Buber; and other activists from Brit Shalom, Ihud, and other peace organizations that opposed the division of the land into two states. These activists, mostly intellectuals of European origin, spoke in the name of humanism, while Ben-Gurion represented the national interest. They talked politics, demanded a more compromising stance, more generosity to the Arabs, while Ben-Gurion talked history and morality. He was troubled, above all, by the fact that his critics regarded their position as more just than his own. He sincerely believed in the justness of Zionism and it was very important to him that the intellectuals also acknowledge this.

Ben-Gurion's Zionism won: After the establishment of the state, there was no longer any point in arguing over the foundations of the Zionist outlook. The dissent was now focused mainly on the wrongs Israel was inflicting on its Arab citizens, which included further deportations and a series of restrictions on civil liberties, such as the military rule imposed on Israeli Arabs during the 1950s by the Ben-Gurion government. In 1956, members of the Israeli Border Police shot dead several dozen Arab-Israeli villagers, residents of Kafr Kassem. They had come home late that day, violating the curfew imposed on their village by the military rule. No other atrocity, not even the massacre perpetrated a quarter of a century later in Sabra and Shatila, aroused such profound shock among the public. This was a turning point in the Israeli press, propelling it several steps ahead toward independent thought, anchored in Western liberal values. Until that point, only a handful had dared criticize the army. The Kafr Kassem massacre shifted the dissent from the margins into the center and, moreover, validated the debate over the occupation of the territories in the Six-Day War of 1967.

The occupation of the Gaza Strip, the West Bank and the Golan Heights flooded Israel with a great wave of messianic patriotism. This atmosphere notwithstanding, the debate over the future of the occupied territories began almost immediately. For the first time since the establishment of the state, the dispute was reignited between those who supported a "Greater Israel" and the continuation of the occupation, and those who advocated partitioning the land. Unlike in the 1940s, it was now the latter who spoke in the name of humanistic justice. This argument still divides Israeli society today, and is not restricted to intellectuals or journalists such as those in this volume.

There is, of course, something deceptive about this voice, and also something frustrating. The deception is in the way official Israeli spokespeople utilize it. Look—they say—how we constantly torment ourselves with pangs of conscience. This is because we are fundamentally good and just; we do not inflict wrongs except when absolutely necessary. The red lines we impose on ourselves, the moral values that guide us even in times of war, attest to the fact that we restrict ourselves to acts whose essence is to protect our existence from our enemies—who do not conduct such moral debates before they strike us because they do not recognize the values of human liberty that direct us. And thus, the voices condemning the occupation are exploited to serve the Israeli myth and, paradoxically, facilitate the perpetuation of the occupation and the expansion of settlements.

All this is made possible because the voices of protest come from people who do not exclude themselves from the Israeli, Zionist collective, but rather try to change it from within. Many are themselves party to the self-righteousness that uses them in order to justify the occupation, the settlements, and the continuous abuse of the Palestinians' human rights. Israeli political Zionism has invented a special term for this dilemma: "shoot and cry." One can withdraw from the Israeli collective and emigrate—a difficult step. One can keep silent—this is also difficult. And so most of us shoot and cry. Most of us serve in the army and condemn the occupation. This is democracy at its finest, we tell ourselves. Many of us console ourselves with private acts of compassion in aid of this or that persecuted Palestinian, usually thanks to our connections in the security establishment: $2,000 raised to purchase a wheelchair for a Palestinian girl, cigarettes sent to a Palestinian prisoner. We all pat each other on the back when we meet at the right cafés and, of course, we all vote for the right parties. Vote and cry.

The Israeli culture of protest is frustrating because it is very difficult to demonstrate its achievements, particularly from a historical perspective. Before the establishment of the state there were two alternatives to the Zionist movement's political program within Jewish public discourse: The ultra-Orthodox opposed the establishment of a state for theological reasons, while the Ihud and Hashomer Hatzair people supported a binational solution—one state for the two peoples, Jewish and Arab. Most Jews objected to both the ultra-Orthodox position and the binational solution; most of the Arabs also opposed the latter. Words written by good guys like Magnes and Buber and Gabriel Stern—kind and true though they may have been—did not prevent the catastrophe that befell the 700,000 Arabs who emigrated, fled or were banished from their homes.

David Ben-Gurion was an extremely authoritarian leader. The Zionist revolution he led went the way of most revolutions and inflicted suffering not only on its Arab enemies but also on its own sons, mainly Jews from Arab countries. But Ben-Gurion's days came to an end and Israel gradually developed a more or less democratic government, with a brave and combatant opposition led by Menachem Begin. Begin attacked the government from the right, but he fought for principles that were also at the core of the left-wing opposition—eradicating military rule and achieving equality for Jewish immigrants from Arab countries. Some of the issues that determined Israel's position were spared criticism; Israel's nuclear project and the work of the Mossad and Shabak [Israel's intelligence agency and General Security Service] were virtually immune. But a study of government documents made public for research reveals that the government did not always ignore criticism, either from the right or the left.

A historical look at Israel's position vis-à-vis the Palestinians also offers hope: Golda Meir refused to recognize the existence of a Palestinian people. Israeli law even prohibited contact with the PLO and Israeli peace activists served prison terms because of their contacts with the organization. Yitzhak Rabin was elected on the basis of a solemn assurance that he would not talk to the PLO; he did. Israel always said it would not withdraw from territories except within the framework of a final agreement like the peace accord with Egypt. Under the Oslo agreement, it withdrew from Palestinian towns without a final peace accord. Moreover, Israel later pulled out of Lebanon unilaterally with no accord whatsoever. It always said it would never agree to the establishment of a Palestinian state. It now does. It said it would never accept a divided rule of Jerusalem. It did. And again, one would like to claim that all this occurred as a result of the Israeli peace movement's activities. Unfortunately, this is very difficult to prove.

Was it the Israeli peace movement that rescued the negotiations with Egypt? Perhaps. Was it the peace movement that led to Oslo and the withdrawal from the territories? Perhaps. Was it the peace movement that caused Israelis to grow weary of the continuing occupation of Lebanon? Perhaps. It was not able to block the settlements, and it is not at all clear whether it indeed created the climate that enabled Oslo or merely reflected this climate. The willingness of so many Israelis to give up the cities that were handed over to the Palestinian Authority under the 1993 Oslo agreement stems from a profound shift in their fundamental perceptions. Many Israelis—now mature and more secure—were no longer living for the collective ideology, but rather for life itself; they were guided not by national togetherness but by a new, very American individualism. They left the national ideology to the right wing. On the same evening that some 60,000 settlers and their supporters took to the streets in Jerusalem to protest the Oslo accord, another 60,000 Israelis gathered in Tel Aviv for a Michael Jackson concert. People who no longer regard themselves as representing exclusive, definitive justice become indifferent not only to the continuation of the settlements, but also to the violation of human rights. The intifada that erupted in September 2000 and, primarily, the terror attacks against densely populated Israeli targets caused many Israelis to revert to a tribal, isolated, emotional, and nationalistic mood. All this creates difficulties for the writers in this volume and limits their influence. The Arabs have a saying for this: The dogs bark and the convoy marches on.

Why, then, do we bark? I suppose that as professional writers most of us believe in the power of words to create a better, more just society, to diminish the wrongs and the violence. We believe in the power of words, at least to a certain extent, because most of us have no other means. The reader will easily observe that the "dogs" in this volume do not bark in one voice. We, too, are capable of biting each other. I suppose not all of us would admit it, but many of us write mainly for ourselves. Life in a society that is not being conducted in a manner that seems right to us, acts of wrongdoing, and sometimes even real war crimes perpetrated in our name arouse in us the need to at least leave behind a testimony that we were against it. In our vanity, we naturally believe that future generations will read our work and it is important to us that they know: We were the good guys on this side of the border.

Gabriel Stern believed the voice he sounded over the pages of *Al Hamishmar* would reach beyond the border, and that when people over there heard there were good guys on this side too, perhaps the danger of war would be minimized. Sometimes I look back on that charming childhood illusion that the good Gabriel bequeathed to me, and I thank him for it.

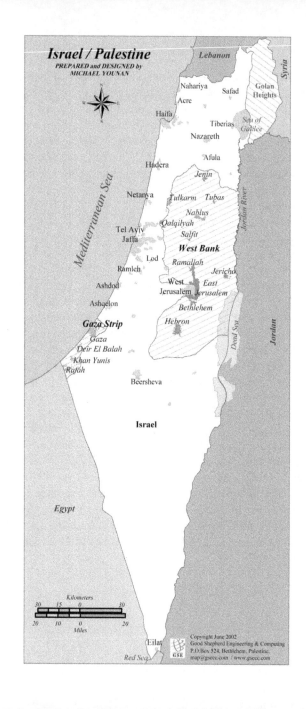

Israel / Palestine

PREPARED and DESIGNED by
MICHAEL YOUNAN

Lebanon

Syria

Nahariya   Safad   Golan Heights

Acre

Haifa

Tiberias   Sea of Galilee

Nazareth

Afula

Hadera

Jenin

Mediterranean Sea

Netanya   Tulkarm   Tubas

Nablus

Qalqilyah

Tel Aviv   Salfit

Jaffa

West Bank

Lod

Ramallah

Jericho

Ramleh

Jordan River

Ashdod   West   East

Jerusalem   Jerusalem

Ashqelon

Bethlehem

Hebron

Gaza Strip

Gaza

Deir El Balah

Khan Yunis

Rafah

Beersheva

Dead Sea

Jordan

Israel

Egypt

Kilometers

30   15   0   30

20   10   0   20

Miles

Eilat

Copyright June 2002
Good Shepherd Engineering & Computing
P.O. Box 524, Bethlehem, Palestine.
map@gsecc.com / www.gsecc.com

Red Sea

GSE

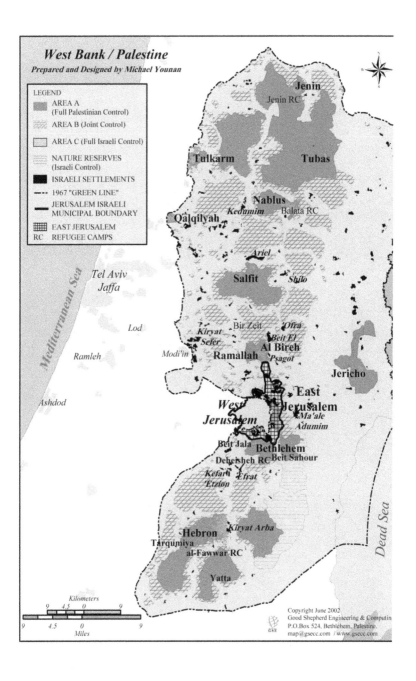

West Bank / Palestine

Prepared and Designed by Michael Younan

LEGEND

AREA A
(Full Palestinian Control)

AREA B (Joint Control)

AREA C (Full Israeli Control)

NATURE RESERVES
(Israeli Control)

ISRAELI SETTLEMENTS

1967 "GREEN LINE"

JERUSALEM ISRAELI
MUNICIPAL BOUNDARY

EAST JERUSALEM

RC   REFUGEE CAMPS

Jenin

Jenin RC

Tulkarm

Tubas

Nablus

Kedumim   Balata RC

Qalqilyah

Ariel

Mediterranean Sea

Tel Aviv
Jaffa

Salfit   Shilo

Lod

Bir Zeit   Ofra

Kiryat   Beit El
Seler   Al Bireh

Ramleh   Modi'in   Ramallah   Psagot

Jericho

Ashdod

East
West   Jerusalem
Jerusalem   Ma'ale
Adumim

Beit Jala   Bethlehem
Dehetsheh RC Beit Sahour

Kefar   Efrat
Etzion

Dead Sea

Kiryat Arba

Hebron

Tarqumiya
al-Fawwar RC

Yatta

Kilometers

9   4.5   0   9

9   4.5   0   9
Miles

Copyright June 2002
Good Shepherd Engineering & Computin
P.O.Box 524, Bethlehem, Palestine.
map@gsecc.com / www.gsecc.com

INTRODUCTION

Anthony Lewis

IN THE DAYS after the 1967 war, when Israel was celebrating its great victory, an Israeli I know warned that triumph could lead to disaster. Capture of the West Bank, East Jerusalem, and the Gaza Strip, he said, would tempt Israel to settle those territories. That would mean colonialism, with all its arrogance and inhumanity. It would undermine the character of Israel.

And it came to pass. The settlement process, carried on for more than three decades, has been sustained by colonial methods: suppressing the local population, seizing land, giving settlers superior legal status. The consequences have been, as my Israeli friend foresaw, corrupting. Now the attempt to extend Israel's dominion threatens its hard-won asset of international legitimacy.

From the day of its rebirth as a state in 1948 Israel had to struggle for acceptance. The Arab world refused to recognize the state or even, for a long time, to call it by its name. Anwar Sadat's visit in 1977 meant so much to Israelis because it represented acceptance. Then, in 1993, the Oslo agreement brought recognition of Israel's legitimacy by the Palestine Liberation Organization.

Palestinian negotiators at Oslo assumed that Israel would gradually abandon the settlements and withdraw to something very like its pre-1967 borders. But Oslo left those steps to further negotiation, and they did not happen. The settlement process continued unchecked after

Oslo. (Peace Now reported in March 2002 that an aerial survey of the West Bank showed thirty-four new settlement sites built in the past year.) More than 200,000 settlers now live in the West Bank. Settlements, some of them small cities, and special highways for the settlers have effectively cut the West Bank into cantons separated by Israeli military forces and checkpoints.

At Camp David in 2000 Prime Minister Ehud Barak offered to withdraw from (by different estimates) between 86 and 91 percent of the West Bank; but his proposal would have left in place barrier settlements and roads that divide the territory. Yasser Arafat said no. Many of us who long for a peaceful end to the conflict thought Arafat's refusal even to explore Barak's offer was a terrible mistake. But in the Palestinians' view, seven years after Oslo they were justifiably skeptical of Israel's willingness ever to give up effective dominion over the occupied territories—ever to allow a genuine Palestinian state free of Israeli barriers.

After Camp David the conflict rose to new levels of bloodshed and destruction. Palestinians carried out appalling acts of terrorism. Hamas's suicide bombers and then elements of Arafat's Fatah targeted civilians in cafés and pizzerias.* Israel retaliated with what in time became its biggest military operation since it invaded Lebanon twenty years ago.

Israeli voters, frightened by terror, brought to power in February 2001 the man who through decades had demonstrated his belief that the answer to Palestinian aspirations is force, Ariel Sharon. Under Sharon as prime minister, Israeli forces laid siege to the West Bank and Gaza, virtually confining the inhabitants to their own villages and

---

* Hamas, the Islamic Resistance Movement, was founded in December 1987 at the beginning of the first intifada. The largest Palestinian Islamic organization, Hamas is not part of the PLO and opposes a two-state solution and recognition of Israel.

  Founded in 1959, the predominantly secular Fatah, the Palestinian Liberation Movement, is the largest organization in the PLO and the dominant group in the Palestinian Authority. The autonomous, activist wing of Fatah, often known as the *tanzim,* has carried out numerous attacks against Israeli soldiers and settlers in the occupied territories; one of its militias, the Al-Aqsa Martyrs Brigades, has extended these attacks to include suicide bombings inside Israel.

towns. (*The Economist* said the siege cut the occupied territories "into 200 disconnected enclaves.") Bulldozers destroyed houses and plowed under olive groves. Israel often responded to acts of terror by punishing people who had not committed the terror, using F-16s to destroy Palestinian Authority police buildings and shelling other sites from naval ships. When terrorists killed Israeli soldiers near the Gaza Strip on January 9, 2002, Israel demolished fifty-four houses in Rafah refugee camp miles away. The siege has wasted the Palestinian economy, increasing unemployment levels to 35 percent in the West Bank and 50 percent in Gaza. A World Bank report at the end of March 2002 said Israeli restrictions had brought the Palestinian economy close to collapse. If the restrictions continue, the bank's director for the area, Nigel Roberts, said, "helplessness, deprivation and hatred will increase."

Recently Kofi Annan wrote to Sharon protesting that Israel had wounded or killed "hundreds of innocent noncombatant civilians," fired on ambulances, and blocked medical access to the wounded. At the climax of Sharon's retaliatory campaign, Israeli forces entered several cities and refugee camps that were supposed to be under Palestinian Authority control, then smashed through the walls of many houses and rounded up hundreds of men for interrogation.

Israel carried out assassinations of alleged Palestinian terrorists, a practice that amounted to conviction and execution without trial. The human rights committee of the Israel Bar Association warned last year that any Israeli who carried out such a killing could be prosecuted for a war crime.

Particular incidents may show the nature of Sharon's policy better than generalities. In the early morning hours of March 8, Israeli tanks and armored troop carriers went into the Deheisheh refugee camp near Bethlehem, firing shells and machine guns to discourage resistance. Issa Faraj was playing with his children in their home when two bullets struck and killed him.

On the same day, March 8, Israeli tanks and troops took over a Lutheran Church school in Bethlehem, the Dar al-Kalima School. It is on a hilltop, and the troops used it as an outpost for surveillance of the city. After a few days they left, and officials of the school reentered it.

They sent an e-mail about what they found: smashed iron external doors and wooden interior ones, crosses taken down and destroyed, graffiti on the walls and other acts of what officials called "pure vandalism and hatred." "What is so offensive to an Israeli soldier about a child's painting of a clock," the e-mail asked, "leading him to throw it on the floor and step on it?"

Sharon's policy of massive retaliation has troubled an increasing number of Israelis, too. In February, more than 200 military reservists said they would refuse to serve their required annual active duty in the occupied Palestinian territories, where they said Israel was "dominating, expelling, starving, and humiliating an entire people." By June almost 300 more reservists had joined them. A thousand former officers, among them generals, called on Israel to withdraw unilaterally from the territories.

Some Israeli and outside analysts suggested that Prime Minister Sharon had a purpose beyond deterring terrorism in his harsh actions: to prevent the resumption of political negotiations with the Palestinians looking to a final peace agreement. As Henry Siegman, a Middle East specialist at the Council on Foreign Relations, put it, "The Sharon government seeks pretexts to avoid a political process, not ways to renew it." Siegman suggested that Sharon's resumption of targeted assassinations during a period when a cease-fire ordered by Arafat last December had dramatically reduced violence was a provocation designed to produce new acts of terror—which it did.

Sharon has always fought the Palestinian vision of a viable state. He played a leading part in the creation of the settlements, and he opposed the Oslo agreement. Uri Avnery, a pro-peace Israeli who over the years has written three biographical essays about Sharon, two with his cooperation, wrote this January that Sharon's "minimum" aim now was "to imprison the Palestinians in several enclaves . . . each one surrounded by settlements, bypass roads and the army. In these big prison camps, the Palestinians will be allowed to 'manage their own affairs,' supplying cheap labor and a captive market. He does not care if they are called 'a Palestinian state.' " Sharon's "maximum" aim, Avnery said, was "to exploit a war situation or a world crisis to expel all Palestinians (including those who are Israeli citizens) from the country."

An Israel that achieved Sharon's "minimum," much less his "maximum," would not be regarded as legitimate by much of the world. That is not just because the goal of Israeli acquisition of territory by force would be deemed impermissible, though several Security Council resolutions make it so. It is because the means Israel has used to maintain its domination of the occupied territories are unacceptable. As it happens, the means are also spectacularly ineffective as a deterrent to terrorism. Every assassination, every smashed refugee camp brings new recruits to the Palestinian organizations that target Israelis. Sharon's strategy, Siegman said, is "a prescription for the 'Lebanonization' of the occupied territories and of Israel's own heartland."

The Bush administration has also brought disaster on itself by its response to Sharon's policy. For a year and more it gave Sharon a blank check, offering no objection to his most brutal actions and supporting his confinement of Arafat in a few square blocks of Ramallah—a step that predictably raised Arafat's approval ratings among Palestinians. U.S. diplomats in Israel surely sent dispatches pointing out the folly of what Israel was doing. Both they and State Department officials in Washington knew of Sharon's well-advertised views. Yet when Sharon said on March 4 that the Palestinians had to be "battered" and "beaten," Secretary of State Colin Powell and President Bush indicated that they were shocked—and began applying pressure on Sharon.

Bush officials were similarly dense in their failure to understand the effect on the Arab world of what was being done to the Palestinians. Night after night Arab television stations showed such scenes as Palestinian children being killed by Israeli weapons—as, again, U.S. diplomats must have reported. Yet Vice President Dick Cheney seemed surprised when he toured the Middle East in late March and government after government told him that U.S. support of Israel's tactics made it impossible to approve of any American action against Iraq. It is hard to know whether the best adjective for American policy toward the conflict over the last year is stupid or shameful.

The Israeli reservists who have refused to serve in the occupied territories call the current phase of the Israeli-Palestinian conflict the "war of the settlements." That is to say that the issue is unambiguous: occupation. There can be peace only when Israel withdraws from the territories it conquered in 1967, leaving an uninterrupted West Bank as part of a viable Palestine. (As Crown Prince Abdullah of Saudi Arabia said in his recent proposal, there could be adjustments to incorporate some settlements into Israel, for example to thicken Israel's narrow waist—if comparable territory, perhaps bordering on the Gaza Strip, were transferred to Palestine.)*

That is the dovish view of how peace can be achieved. Everyone knows what a final agreement would look like. The borders of the new Palestine would be something like what President Clinton proposed following Camp David—and what the two sides discussed at Taba in Egypt in January 2001—including the West Bank, all of the Gaza Strip, and the predominantly Palestinian parts of East Jerusalem. The other claim that Arafat made at Camp David—a right of return for Palestinian refugees—could not be included except in some modest symbolic way, controlled by Israel. Otherwise, Israel would soon become another Palestinian state. As Sari Nusseibeh, the philosopher who is Arafat's representative in Jerusalem, has said, the idea of a mass return is inconsistent with the Palestinian leadership's endorsement at Oslo of a two-state solution: Israeli and Palestinian states, living side by side in peace. In February, in an Op-Ed piece for the *New York Times*, Arafat called for "creative solutions to the plight of the refugees while respecting Israel's demographic concerns." That sounds reasonable, but exactly what he means can emerge only in a negotiation.

The Israeli right wing, and influential American conservative supporters of Israel, do not believe in the premises of the two-state solution. They contend that Arafat has not really accepted Israel's right to exist. They argue that Palestinians, most of them, want not just to reclaim the occupied territories but to destroy Israel. So they would make no more concessions to the Palestinians. They would rely on force to keep what Israel has now. Benjamin Netanyahu, the former prime min-

---

* Abdullah's proposal, commonly known as the Saudi plan, was adopted unanimously at the Arab League summit in Beirut in March 2002. It offers full normalization of relations between the Arab nations and Israel in return for full Israeli withdrawal from the occupied territories as called for in UN Security Council Resolutions 242 and 338.

ister who threatens Sharon from the right, would be even harsher. And to his right there are those whose solution is to "transfer" all the Palestinians out of Palestine.

A significant recent recruit to the right's pessimism about Palestinian intentions is Benny Morris, an Israeli history professor who outraged conservatives by writing, in a 1988 book, that the thousands of Arabs who fled the new Israel in 1948 in large part did so not because of broadcast advice from the Arab world—as the traditional Israeli thesis had it—but because Israeli fighters forced or frightened them into fleeing. This February, writing in London's *Guardian,* Morris did not renounce that view of history.* But he had come to believe, he said, that today the Palestinian leadership really denies Israel's legitimacy. "This question of legitimacy," he wrote, "seemingly put to rest by the Israeli-Egyptian and Israeli-Jordanian peace treaties, is at the root of current Israeli despair and my own 'conversion.' "

Morris called Arafat "an inveterate liar." For a few years after Oslo in 1993, he said, Arafat and the PLO "seemed to have acquiesced in the idea of a compromise. But since 2000 the dominant vision of a 'Greater Palestine' has surged back to the fore." Lately, he noted, Arafat has taken to questioning whether there was ever a Jewish temple in Jerusalem. He thus refuses, Morris said, "to recognize the history and reality of the 3,000-year-old Jewish connection to the land of Israel."

Then, in his article, Morris took a sharp turn. "Don't get me wrong," he wrote. "I favor an Israeli withdrawal from the territories—the semi-occupation is corrupting and immoral, and alienates Israel's friends abroad. . . ." But Morris said he did not believe a two-state solution would last. Arafat was incapable, he wrote, of really giving up the right of return—of looking the refugees in the eye and telling them, "I have signed away your birthright, your hope, your dream." So in time there would be more terrorism, an Israeli military response, and, in the end,

---

* See Benny Morris, "Peace? No Chance," *Guardian,* February 21, 2002. Avi Shlaim's response, "A Betrayal of History," was published in the *Guardian* on February 22 and is reprinted in this volume on page 45.

one state in all of Palestine that would be predominantly either Jewish or Palestinian.

I can agree with some of what Morris says. Yasser Arafat is not the leader Palestinians deserve; he has not been able to make the transition from guerrilla chieftain to statesman, to bring his people with him, to inspire the trust of his one-time enemies. His Palestinian Authority is undemocratic and corrupt. His denial of the existence of the Jewish Temple in Jerusalem is despicable.

Arafat allowed terrorism to flourish to a point where he probably could not stop it when he wanted to. The terrible suicide bombing that killed twenty-nine Israelis at a Seder in Netanya on March 27, for example, was against Arafat's interest in the maneuvering over a cease-fire and over peace prospects more broadly.

In the end, though, it seems to me, the pessimists have no solution. Military force to keep control of the West Bank has been tried and failed. The settlements do not give Israel security "depth," as the right wing likes to say, but put heavy burdens on the Israel Defense Forces. Think of the troops committed and the lives lost to protect the Israeli settlements that take up a quarter of the stiflingly overcrowded Gaza Strip. It is overwhelmingly clear now that there is no hope of ending terrorism until the Palestinians see a realistic prospect of negotiating a viable state of their own.

A solution along the lines of Crown Prince Abdullah's proposal would entail risks for Israel, of course. Suicide attacks might still continue. But such a solution is a better gamble than a policy that has not stopped terrorism, that has corrupted Israel's values, and that has aroused antagonism toward Israel in much of the world. Zionism, with its noble goal of a Jewish national homeland, faces the ultimate test of its legitimacy: whether it will accept limits, accept that another people has a legitimate claim to a national home in Palestine.

What began on March 29 turned into a large-scale Israeli military assault on the Palestinians. The target, Prime Minister Sharon repeatedly said, was the "infrastructure of terror"; alleged terrorists were arrested, and arms and explosives seized. But the extent of the physical destruction by Israeli forces made clear the real purpose of the operation: to destroy the Palestinian Authority and the structure of a future Palestinian state.

Israeli soldiers took over an educational television station, threw its computers out the windows, and destroyed the broadcasting machinery. They removed the computerized records of the school system and other purely civil offices of the Authority. They systematically destroyed the buildings of the Palestinian police. They blew up civilian homes, water lines, and electric lines.

The operation won wide support from Israelis as an entirely understandable act of revenge against the terror of the suicide bombings. But its effect was to continue the policy that guarantees Palestinian hatred and Israeli insecurity: the policy of colonizing the occupied territories and making Israel's effective control of Palestinian land permanent.

As Michael Ben-Yair says in the essay that follows, it is a policy that destroys the moral basis of Israeli society.

Part One

THE SETTING

1

THE SIX-DAY WAR'S SEVENTH DAY

Michael Ben-Yair

THE ZIONIST DREAM'S realization and the Jewish people's national rebirth through the creation of Israel were achieved not because of the Jewish side's superior number of tanks, planes, or other means of aggression. The State of Israel was born because the Zionist movement realized it must find a solution to the Jews' persecution and because the enlightened world recognized the need for that solution.

The enlightened world's recognition of the solution's moral justification was an important, principal factor in Israel's creation. In other words, Israel was established on a clear, recognized moral base. Without such a moral base, it is doubtful whether the Zionist idea would have become a reality.

The Six-Day War was forced upon us; however, the war's seventh day, which began on June 12, 1967 and has continued to this day, is the product of our choice. We enthusiastically chose to become a colonial society, ignoring international treaties, expropriating lands, transferring settlers from Israel to the occupied territories, engaging in theft and finding justification for all these activities. Passionately desiring to keep the occupied territories, we developed two judicial systems: one—progressive, liberal—in Israel and the other—cruel, injurious—in the occupied territories. In effect, we established an apartheid regime in the occupied territories immediately following their capture. That oppressive regime exists to this day.

The Six-Day War's seventh day has transformed us from a moral society, sure of the justice of Israel's creation, into a society that oppresses another people, preventing it from realizing its legitimate national aspirations. The Six-Day War's seventh day has transformed us from a just society into an unjust one, prepared to expand its control atop another nation's ruins. The discarding of our moral foundation has hurt us as a society, reinforcing the arguments of the world's hostile elements and sowers of evil and intensifying their influence.

The intifada is the Palestinian people's war of national liberation. Historical processes teach us that no nation is prepared to live under another's domination and that a suppressed people's war of national liberation will inevitably succeed. We understand this point but choose to ignore it. We are prepared to engage in confrontation to prevent a historical process, although we are well aware that this process is anchored in the moral justification behind every people's war of national liberation and behind its right to self-determination, and although we are well aware that this process will attain its inevitable goal.

This is the background of the difficult testimony we have received about actions of Israel Defense Forces personnel in the occupied territories. No need to repeat the details of the painful phenomena entailed in the occupation regime and in our battle to prolong it. Suffice it to recall the killing of little children fleeing for safety; the executions, without trial, of wanted persons who were not on their way to launch a terrorist act; and the encirclements, closures and roadblocks that have turned the lives of millions into a nightmare. Even if all these actions stem from our need to defend ourselves under an occupation's conditions, the occupation's non-existence would render them unnecessary. Thus, a black flag hovers over these actions.*

This is a harsh reality that is causing us to lose the moral base of our

* "Black flag" was the term used by Judge Binyamin Halevy in a 1958 trial of members of the Border Police, who shot and killed nearly fifty civilians from the Israeli Arab village of Kafr Kassem in October 1956 as they returned home from work, unaware that their village had been placed under curfew at the start of the Sinai War. Defining the nature of an illegal order not to be obeyed, Halevy wrote, "The hallmark of manifest illegality is that it must wave like a black flag over the given order."

existence as a free, just society and to jeopardize Israel's long-term survival. Israel's security cannot be based only on the sword; it must rather be based on our principles of moral justice and on peace with our neighbors—those living next door and those living a little farther away. An occupation regime undermines those principles of moral justice and prevents the attainment of peace. Thus, that regime endangers Israel's existence.

It is against this background that one must view the refusal of IDF reservist officers and soldiers to serve in the territories. In their eyes, the occupation regime is evil and military service in the occupied territories, which places soldiers in situations forcing them to commit immoral acts, is evil. According to their conscience, they cannot be party to such acts. Thus, their refusal to serve is an act of conscience that is justified and recognized in every democratic regime. History's verdict will be that their refusal was the act that restored our moral backbone.

March 3, 2002

2

THE SECOND HALF OF 1948

Tanya Reinhart

OFFICIAL DECLARATIONS AND many reports in the Israeli media indicate that the military and political leadership are aiming, eventually, at a total destruction of the Palestinian Authority, and, with it, the Oslo process which is now considered by most of them to be a "historical mistake." What can they be after? Let us trace some of the background of this development.

Ever since the 1967 occupation, the military and political elites (which have always been closely intertwined in Israel) deliberated over the question of how to keep maximum land with minimum Palestinian population. The leaders of the 1948 generation—Yigal Allon, Ariel Sharon, Moshe Dayan, Yitzhak Rabin and Shimon Peres—were raised on the myth of redemption of land. But a simple solution of annexation of the occupied territories would have turned the occupied Palestinians into Israeli citizens, and this would have caused what has been labeled the "demographic problem"—the fear that the Jewish majority could not be preserved. Therefore, two basic conceptions were developed.

The Allon plan consisted of annexation of 35–40 percent of the territories to Israel, and self-rule or partnership in a confederation of the rest, the land on which the Palestinians actually live. In the eyes of its proponents, this plan represented a necessary compromise, because they believed it was impossible to repeat the 1948 "solution" of mass expulsion, either for moral considerations or because world opinion would not allow this to happen again.

The second conception, whose primary spokesman was Sharon, assumed that it was possible to find more acceptable and sophisticated ways to achieve a 1948-style solution—it was only necessary to find another state for the Palestinians; "Jordan is Palestine" was the phrase that Sharon coined. So future arrangements should guarantee that as many Palestinians as possible would move there. For Sharon, this was part of a more global worldview, by which Israel would establish "new orders" in the region—a view he experimented with in the Lebanon war of 1982.

In Oslo, the Allon plan triumphed, where gradually it became apparent that it was even possible to extend the "Arab-free" areas. In practice, the Palestinians have already been dispossessed of half of their lands, which are now state lands, security zones and "land reserves for the settlements." However, it appeared that Israel would be satisfied with that, and would allow the PA to run the enclaves in which the Palestinians still reside, in some form of self-rule which would even be called a Palestinian "state." The security establishment expressed full confidence in the ability of the Palestinian security forces—which were created and trained in cooperation with the Israelis—to control the frustration of the Palestinians and protect the security of the settlers and the Israeli home front.

But the victory of the Allon plan wasn't complete. Even the little that the Palestinians did get seemed too much to some in military circles, whose most vocal spokesman in the early years of Oslo was then-Chief of Staff Ehud Barak. Another consistent voice is that of Major General Moshe (Bugi) Ya'alon, who is also known for his connections with the settlers.* Contradicting the position of the security services (Shin Bet, or Shabak) and the many media reports that praised the security cooperation between Israel and the Palestinian Authority, Ya'alon claimed in a cabinet meeting in September 1997, and later, that "Arafat is giving a green light to terror."

The objection to Oslo in military circles was based on the view that it would be impossible to maintain such an arrangement in the long term. If the Palestinians have a political infrastructure and armed

---

* Ya'alon was scheduled to become IDF Chief of Staff in July 2002.

forces, it was thought, they would eventually try to rebel. Therefore, the only way was to overthrow the Palestinian Authority and the whole Oslo conception. The first step on this route was to convince the public that Arafat is still a terrorist and is personally responsible for the acts of all groups, from the Islamic Jihad to Hizbollah.*

During Barak's days in office, Ya'alon became one of his closest confidants in the restricted military team that Barak assembled. The same team was prepared already at the beginning of the intifada for a total attack on the Palestinian Authority, on both the military and the propaganda levels. On the latter, this included the "White Book" on the crimes of Arafat and the PA. This is the same team that is now briefing the political level, as well as U.S. representatives, and is responsible for the dominance of the call for toppling the PA.

But what can they have in mind as a replacement for the Oslo arrangements? One wave of rumors is that the IDF plans to reinstall Israeli military rule. But this does not make any sense as a long-term plan. The Oslo agreements were conceived precisely because that system could no longer work. The burden of policing the territories was much too heavy on the army, the reserves, and Israeli society, and the IDF's success in preventing terror was, in fact, much lower than that of the PA in later years. After the Lebanon experience, and after the seven years of Oslo, during which Israeli society got used to the idea that the occupation comes for free, with the PA taking care of the settlers' security, it is hard to imagine that anyone believes a pre-Oslo arrangement can be reinstalled.

It is hard to avoid the conclusion that after thirty years of occupation, the two options competing in the Israeli power system are precisely the same as those set by the generation of 1948: apartheid (the Allon-Oslo plan), or transfer—the mass evacuation of Palestinian resi-

---

* Islamic Jihad, which was formed in the early 1980s by militant dissenters from the Muslim Brotherhood, advocates an Islamic state in all of Palestine. Hizbollah (the Party of God) arose among Lebanon's Shiite Muslim population in the wake of Israel's 1982 invasion. Inspired by the 1979 Iranian revolution and formed under the influence of Iranian Revolutionary Guards, Hizbollah led the victorious guerrilla resistance against the Israeli occupation and is now a political party represented in Lebanon's Parliament.

dents, as happened in 1948 (the Sharon plan). Those pushing for the destruction of the Oslo infrastructure may still believe that under the appropriate conditions of regional escalation, the transfer plan will become feasible.

In modern times, wars aren't openly started over land and water. In order to attack, you first need to prove that the enemy isn't willing to live in peace and is threatening your very existence. Barak managed to do that. Now conditions are ripe for executing Sharon's plan, or for—as Ya'alon put it in November 2000—"the second half of 1948."

Before we reach that dark line, there is one option that has never been tried: Get out of the occupied territories immediately.

June 10, 2001

3

THE KEY TO PEACE:
DISMANTLING THE MATRIX OF CONTROL

Jeff Halper

IN THE COMPLEX and tragic situation in which Palestinians and Israelis currently find themselves, two things seem equally evident: First, a viable and truly sovereign Palestinian state alongside Israel is an absolute prerequisite for a just and lasting peace; and second, Israel needs a Palestinian state. Without a Palestinian state Israel faces what it considers two unacceptable options. If it annexes the occupied territories and grants citizenship to their three million Palestinian inhabitants, it creates de facto a binational state of five million Jews and four million Palestinians (not counting the refugees), an option that would end the Zionist enterprise. If it continues its occupation, it inevitably creates a system of outright apartheid, an untenable option in the long run.

A Palestinian state thus appears to be indispensable for both Israel and the Palestinians. So what's the problem? Why did a decade of negotiations from Madrid and Oslo to Camp David and Taba end in such dismal failure, indeed, in an intifada? What must be done, not only to restart the peace process, but to ensure that it concludes with a just peace—not simply security for Israel but also a truly sovereign and viable state for the Palestinians?

Putting the issue of the refugees aside for the moment, the answer to these questions depends on whether the Palestinians succeed in dismantling the matrix of control Israel has laid over the occupied territories since 1967. The issue before us—the issue separating a just peace from an imposed one, a sovereign Palestinian state from a bantustan—has to do not only with territory but with control. One indisputable fact that has accompanied the entire peace process is that Israel simply would not relinquish control voluntarily over the West Bank and East Jerusalem. It would not relinquish the core of its settlement system, or control of the West Bank aquifers, or sway over the area's economy or its "security arrangements" extending over the entire Palestinian area.

From Israel's point of view, then, the trick was to find an arrangement that would leave it in control, but relieve it of the Palestinian population—a kind of occupation-by-consent. This was the essence of the "take it or leave it" offer Barak and Clinton made at Camp David (the Palestinians left it), as well as that of the Taba negotiations in January 2001. The popular impression has it that at Camp David Barak made a "generous offer" of 95 percent of the West Bank, plus considerable parts of East Jerusalem and all of Gaza, and that the Palestinians made a historic mistake in rejecting it. This has let Israel off the hook; public opinion in both Israel and abroad (particularly the United States) supports Israeli suppression of Palestinian resistance to the ongoing and constantly expanding occupation. After all, asked Foreign Minister Shimon Peres, what are the Palestinians resisting? Even the moderate Israeli left blames the Palestinians for spoiling the peace process. It is a neat formula. "They" spurned Barak's generous offer and responded with violence, the intifada. We, the Israelis, did our part. We were forthcoming. They are not ready for peace, do not want peace, are not partners for peace, want only to throw us all into the sea. We are OK, we tried to give them a state. They are to blame for everything. They deserve anything they get. We are not responsible. "We," Sharon repeats tirelessly, "are the victims."

THE MATRIX OF CONTROL:
RENDERING THE OCCUPATION INVISIBLE

East Asians have a board game called Go. Unlike the Western game of chess, where two opponents try to defeat each other by taking off pieces, the aim of Go is completely different. You win not by defeating but by immobilizing your opponent by controlling key points on the matrix. This strategy was used effectively during the war in Vietnam, where small forces of Viet Cong were able to pin down and virtually paralyze some half-million American soldiers possessing overwhelming firepower.

Israel has employed a similar strategy against the Palestinians in the territories. Since 1967 it has put into place a matrix of control. Like the Go board, Israel's matrix of control is an integrated system designed (1) to allow Israel to control every aspect of Palestinian life in the occupied territories, while (2) lowering Israel's military profile so as to give the impression that what Palestinians refer to as occupation is merely proper administration, and (3) that Israel's military repression is merely self-defense against an aggressive Palestinian people endeavoring to expel it, yet (4) carving out just enough space in the form of disconnected enclaves to establish a dependent Palestinian mini-state that will relieve Israel of the Palestinian population while (5) forcing the Palestinians to despair of ever achieving a viable and truly sovereign state and thereby accept any settlement offered by Israel.

The matrix of control not only lays a web of constraints over every aspect of Palestinian life in the daily realm, it also hides the occupation behind a facade of laws, planning procedures and Kafkaesque administration. It casts the occupation as "proper administration," "upholding the law," "keeping public order," and, of course, "security." In normal times (when active Palestinian resistance can be stifled), its outward appearance is legal and bureaucratic. For example, Israel's military government is called the Civil Administration, even though it is headed by a colonel under the strict authority of the Ministry of Defense, and is bound by the orders of the general commanding the Central Front. Over the long term it employs a mix of attrition, suppression, delegitimization and diplomatic isolation to achieve its goal of compelling the Palestinians to submit to an Israeli-controlled mini-state.

The matrix operates on three interlocking levels:

Military Controls and Military Strikes
Outright military actions, including attacks on civilian population centers and the Palestinian infrastructure, especially evident during the

two intifadas (1987–1993; 2000–present), are not Israel's preferred means of control. They are too brutal, too evident, and they generate both internal and foreign opposition. But military force is used effectively and with impunity to suppress resistance to the occupation and as a deterrent ("teaching the Palestinians a lesson," conveying a "message"). Although justified by security concerns, in the long term Israel prefers to control the Palestinians administratively—through the issuance of thousands of military orders and by "creating facts on the ground."

Extensive use is made of collaborators and undercover *mustarabi* army units. The dependency that Israel's stifling administration engenders turns thousands of Palestinians into unwilling (and occasionally willing) collaborators. Simple things such as obtaining a driver's or business license, a work permit, a permit to build a house, a travel document or permission to receive hospital care in Israel or abroad is often conditioned on supplying information to the security services. So effective is this that Israel can locate and assassinate ("targeted liquidations") Palestinian figures in their cars or even in telephone booths. But collaboration also undermines Palestinian society by diffusing fear and distrust.

Mass arrests and administrative detention are also common features of the military side of the matrix of control. In the March and April 2002 raids on West Bank cities, towns, villages and refugee camps, about 3,000 people were detained, 280 of them held in administrative detention—which can last for months or years—without being either charged or tried.

Creating Facts on the Ground

Massive expropriation of Palestinian land is an ongoing phenomenon. Since 1967 Israel has expropriated for settlements, highways, bypass roads, military installations, nature preserves and infrastructure some 24 percent of the West Bank, 89 percent of Arab East Jerusalem and 25 percent of Gaza.

More than 200 settlements have been constructed in the occupied territories; 400,000 Israelis have moved across the 1967 boundaries (200,000 in the West Bank, 200,000 in East Jerusalem and 6,000 in

Gaza). Although settlements take up only 1.6 percent of the West Bank, fully 42 percent is under the effective control of Israel's local and regional councils or the military. Besides settling the "Greater Land of Israel," a key goal of the settlement enterprise has been to foreclose the establishment of a viable Palestinian state (or, for some, any Palestinian state) by carving the occupied territories into dozens of enclaves surrounded, isolated and controlled by Israeli settlements, infrastructure and military. While leaving enough land free for a Palestinian ministate of greater or smaller proportions, the settlement network ensures effective Israeli control over Palestinian movement and construction.

While a number of Israeli highways were built in the occupied territories before the Oslo accords, construction of a massive system of twenty-nine highways and bypass roads, funded entirely by the United States (at a cost of $3 billion), was begun only at the start of the peace process. Designed to link settlements, to create barriers to Palestinian movement, and, in the end, to incorporate the West Bank into Israel proper, this project, which takes up an additional 17 percent of West Bank land, contributed materially to the creation of "facts on the ground" that prejudiced the negotiations.

Another mechanism of division and control that came into being with the signing of the Oslo II agreement in 1995 was the further carving of the occupied territories into Areas A, B and C (in the West Bank),* H-1 and H-2 in Hebron, Yellow, Green, Blue and White in Gaza, Israeli-controlled "nature reserves," closed military areas, security zones, and "open green spaces" which restricted Palestinian construction in more than half of East Jerusalem. This system, which has become ever more formalized and controlled, confines Palestinians to an archipelago of some 190 islands encircled by the Israeli matrix. Israel formally controls 60 percent of the West Bank (Area C), 60 percent of Gaza and all of East Jerusalem. Its frequent incursions into Palestinian territory and its virtual destruction of the Palestinian Authority in

---

* In Area A the Palestinian Authority had full administrative and security control; in Area B the PA had administrative control and Israel had security control; and in Area C Israel had full control. At the time of the 2000 Camp David talks, Area A comprised less than 18 percent of the West Bank.

March and April 2002 have left it, however, in de facto control of the entire country. Hundreds of permanent, semi-permanent and "spontaneous" checkpoints and border crossings severely limit and control Palestinian movement.

Construction of seven (of a planned twelve) industrial parks on the seam between the occupied territories and Israel give new life to isolated settlements while robbing Palestinian cities, with which they are in direct competition for workers and markets, of their own economic vitality. The industrial parks exploit cheap Palestinian labor while denying Palestinian workers access to Israel. They also allow Israel's most polluting and least profitable industries to continue dumping their industrial wastes into the West Bank and Gaza.

Israel's matrix of control extends underground as well, using settlement sites to maintain control over the main aquifers of the occupied territories and other vital natural resources.

Even seemingly innocuous holy places such as Rachel's Tomb in Bethlehem, the Cave of the Patriarchs in Hebron, sites in and around Jerusalem and Joseph's Tomb in Nablus (abandoned in the fall of 2000 under fire) serve as pretexts for maintaining an Israeli "security presence," and hence military control reinforced by settlement.

Bureaucracy, Planning and Law

These are the most subtle of control mechanisms, entangling Palestinians in a tight web of restrictions and triggering sanctions whenever Palestinians try to expand their life space. They include orders issued by the military commanders of the West Bank and Gaza (some 2,000 since 1967), supplemented by Civil Administration policies, that replace local civil law with procedures designed to strengthen Israeli political control.

Since the start of the peace process a permanent closure has been laid over the West Bank and Gaza, severely restricting the numbers of Palestinian workers allowed into Israel and impoverishing the Palestinian community, whose own infrastructure has been kept underdeveloped. The closure has many forms. It obtains between Israel and the occupied territories, between Areas A, B and C and even within Palestinian enclaves. It can take a more open form one day (a "breathing closure") and prevent any movement the next (a "strangling closure"). It may be permanent (as between Israel and the territories) or may be decreed for a particular military or security purpose of undetermined length and severity (as in the siege of Palestinian cities, towns, and villages). The closure in all its forms prevents the development of a coherent Palestinian economy. Discriminatory and often arbitrary systems of work, entrance, and travel permits further restrict freedom of movement both within the country and abroad.

In mid-May 2002 the government announced the formal division of the West Bank into eight cantons (Jenin, Nablus, Tulkarm, Qalqilyah, Ramallah, Jericho, Bethlehem, and Hebron), with movement among them allowed only by permits from the Civil Administration. This represents nothing less than the reoccupation of areas A and B, and adds yet another layer of control.

Given Israel's goal of controlling the entire country and its "demographic problem" (Palestinians will soon outnumber Jews in the area between the Jordan River and the Mediterranean Sea), policies of displacement are actively pursued: exile and deportation; revoking of residency rights; economic impoverishment; land expropriation, house demolitions and other means of making life in the occupied territories so unbearable that it will induce "voluntary" Palestinian emigration. Schemes of "transfer" have become a common and acceptable part of Israeli political discourse. (Two parties that have served in Sharon's government, the National Union Party of the assassinated minister Rehavam Ze'evi and Avigdor Lieberman's "Israel Is Our Home," promote transfer as their main political program.)

Zoning and planning policies are ideal vehicles for rendering the occupation invisible, since they are couched in supposedly neutral terms and professional jargon but serve Israel's political ends by obstructing the natural development of Palestinian towns and villages. Central to this system is the restrictive use of building permits, reinforced by house demolitions, arrests and fines for "illegal" building, and daily harassment by Israeli building inspectors. While the Palestinian population is being confined to small enclaves, planning for Israeli expansion employs broad master plans for the settlements. Within this framework Israel can cynically claim that its settlement building is "frozen" and that it is only "thickening" existing ones for purposes of "natural growth," while in fact small settlements often give rise to large settlement-cities, which do not count because they share an existing master plan.

Administrative restrictions intrude into every corner of Palestinian life, enveloping the average person in a web of constraints and controls. Severe restrictions on the planting and sale of crops hit an already impoverished population hard, especially when combined with Israel's practice of uprooting hundreds of thousands of olive and fruit trees since 1967, either to clear land for settlement activity or for "security" purposes. Licensing and inspection of Palestinian businesses is also an effective means of stunting the local economy and extending Israeli political control.

BARAK'S "GENEROUS OFFER" IN THE LIGHT OF THE MATRIX OF CONTROL

We are now in a position to evaluate the meaning of Barak's "generous offer" using control, viability and sovereignty as our measures, rather than solely territory. This is no mere academic exercise. The contention that Israel made far-reaching concessions to the Palestinians and that their rebuff with violence led to the breakdown of the peace process and our present state of conflict underpins, as we have mentioned, popular views in Israel and abroad that the Palestinians are to blame and that Israel's policies of repression are justified. It certainly created the political climate in Israel and the United States that permitted the ferocious incursions into the Jenin refugee camp, Nablus, Ramallah and other Palestinian cities and towns in April–May 2002. Since 95 percent appears on the surface to be generous indeed (who, after all, gets 100 percent in negotiations?), those trying to explain why it was not a good deal are at a distinct disadvantage. The ability to persuade decision makers and the public that the Palestinians were right, and to ensure a peace process in the future that will not repeat the mistakes of Oslo, hangs in the balance.

What, then, of this "generous offer"? First, there never was an Israeli offer, and Israel never proposed to relinquish 95 percent of the West Bank. The last concrete negotiations that took place between Israelis and Palestinians were at Camp David, where Israel was prepared to relinquish some 85 percent of the West Bank and disconnected pieces of East Jerusalem. The subsequent talks at Taba, in January 2001, took place at a desperate time for Barak, when he knew he would lose the upcoming February election. Nonetheless, the Taba discussions were promising. The Israeli delegation came prepared to talk about conceding 93 percent of the West Bank—with the Palestinians counter-proposing 97 percent. But they were not talking about the same land. Because Israel does not consider East Jerusalem and "No Man's Land" around Latrun as part of the West Bank, but does include part of the Dead Sea, Barak's 93 percent was actually more like 88 percent of the actual Palestinian territory.

Some significant gains were made at Taba. Israel relinquished its claim to the Jordan Valley (with the proviso that early-warning stations would be established there, and that Israel reserved the right to unilaterally deploy troops there if it perceived a security threat), territory was conceded (though an Israel-controlled Greater Jerusalem would have to be accepted by the Palestinians), the settlement blocs were reduced in size, and Israel would relinquish extra-territorial control of most of its bypass road system. The Palestinians gained a greater degree of territorial contiguity and control of their borders, though not of their water resources.

However, it is a major fallacy to equate territory with sovereignty. Although gaining control of 95 percent or 88 percent of the territory is important—especially if the territory is contiguous—it does not necessarily equal a truly sovereign state. For the sake of argument, let's adopt the best-case scenario—that at Taba Barak, in fact, made a "generous offer" of 95 percent of the West Bank, all of Gaza and parts of East Jerusalem to the Palestinians. Would that have led to a sovereign and viable Palestinian state? Would it have dismantled Israel's matrix of control? The answer, I would suggest, is no.

If anything, Taba revealed how much Israel could relinquish and still retain effective control over the entire country. It revealed those essential elements of the matrix of control that any foreseeable Israeli government would seek to retain. Examined closely, this is what the "generous offer" in fact offered:

Consolidation of Strategic Settlement Blocs

In the mid-1990s Israel began a major strengthening and consolidation of its settlement presence. In order to avoid international opposition to the establishment of new settlements, the government shifted to building new settlements within the expansive master plans around each settlement. It also began to merge discrete settlements into large settlement blocs. Although the fate of some of these blocs remains uncertain (the Jordan Valley settlements, for example, as well as the Kiryat Arba bloc near Hebron and settlements in heavily populated Palestinian areas), Israel is unmoving in its insistence on retaining three large blocs comprising today some 150,000—or 80 percent—of the West Bank settlers. (Barak often said that he strove for a peace "that even the settlers would be happy with.") These blocs are:

1. The city of Ariel and its surrounding Western Samaria bloc, which control a strategic area on the western side of the West Bank, seriously compromising territorial contiguity and the coherent flow of people and goods between the major Palestinian towns of Qalqilyah, Nablus, and Ramallah. It would also severely restrict the urban development of the Qalqilyah area. No less important than its strategic location on the ground is Ariel's location vis-à-vis Palestinian resources under the ground: The Ariel bloc sits atop the major aquifer of the West Bank and would control the flow and distribution of water.

2. The central Givat Ze'ev/Pisgat Ze'ev/Ma'ale Adumim (and perhaps Beit El) bloc, which stretches across much of the central West Bank from the Modi'in area in the west to within twenty kilometers of the Jordan River in the east. It effectively divides the West Bank in two, compelling north-south Palestinian traffic (especially from Ramallah to the Bethlehem and Hebron areas) to

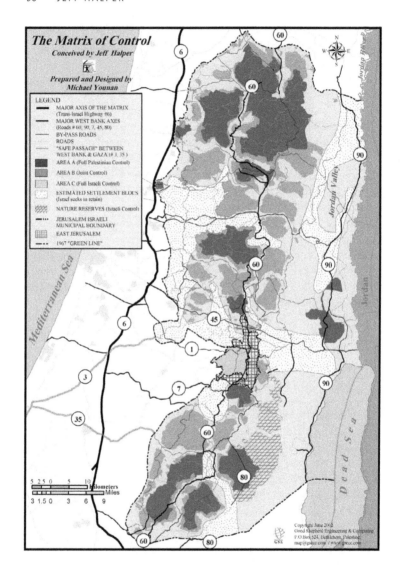

pass through Israeli territory—the funnel-like Eastern Ring Road. It also keeps the Palestinians of the West Bank far from Jerusalem, isolating the 200,000 Palestinians of East Jerusalem from their wider state and society, and cutting the natural urban link between Jerusalem and Ramallah. In terms of viability, this bloc, a main component of Israeli Greater Jerusalem, constitutes the greatest threat to a coherent Palestinian state.

3. The Efrat/Etzion/Beitar Illit bloc to the southwest of Jerusalem (connected through Gilo, Har Homa and the Eastern Ring Road–Road 7 complex to the Ma'ale Adumim Bloc), which severs any coherent connection between the major cities of Bethlehem and Hebron, as well as traffic using the "safe passage" from Gaza. This bloc forces Palestinians moving between these areas to use Israeli-controlled "security" roads passing through dense areas of settlement, continually exposed to disruption and closure. It locks in Bethlehem to the extent of preventing its normal urban development. And, like the Ariel Bloc, it sits astride and brings under Israeli control a major West Bank aquifer.

Emergence of a Metropolitan (Israeli) Jerusalem

The ring roads and major highways being built through and around Jerusalem are intended to create a regional infrastructure of control, turning Jerusalem from a city into a metropolitan region. Metropolitan Jerusalem covers a huge area. Its boundaries, incorporating a full 10 percent of the West Bank (440 square kilometers), stretch from Beit Shemesh west of Jerusalem up through Kiryat Sefer until and including Ramallah, then southeast through Ma'ale Adumim almost to the Jordan River, then turning southwest to encompass Beit Sahour, Bethlehem, Efrat and the Etzion Bloc, then west again through Beitar Illit and Tsur Hadassah to Beit Shemesh. It also provides a crucial link to Kiryat Arba and the settlements in and around Hebron. In many ways Metropolitan Jerusalem *is* the occupation. Within its limits are found 75 percent of the West Bank settlers and the major centers of Israeli construction.

By employing a regional approach to the planning of highways, industrial parks and urban settlements, an Israeli-controlled metropolis

The Three Jerusalems: Municipal, Greater and Metropolitan
Prepared and Designed by Michael Younan

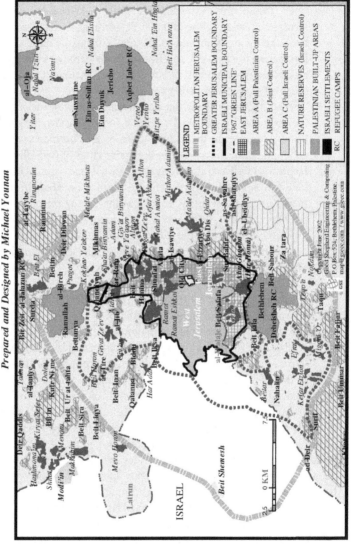

can emerge whose very power as a center of urban activity, employment and transportation will render political boundaries, such as those between Jerusalem and Ramallah or Jerusalem and Bethlehem, irrelevant. A good example of how this is already happening is the new industrial park, Sha'ar Binyamin, now being built at the "Eastern Gate" to Metropolitan Jerusalem, southeast of Ramallah. In terms of Israeli control this industrial park provides an economic anchor to settlements—Kokhav Ya'akov, Tel Zion, Ma'ale Mikhmas, Almon, Psagot, Adam, all the way to Beit El and Ofra—that otherwise would be isolated from the Israeli and Jerusalem economy. More to the point, it robs Ramallah of its economic dynamism, taking jobs and perhaps even sites from Palestinian industry that would otherwise be located in or around Ramallah. Again, looking at Israel's strategy from the point of view of control rather than territory, metropolitan Jerusalem virtually empties a Palestinian state of its meaning in terms of viability and sovereignty.

An East Jerusalem Patchwork

Between the negotiations at Camp David and Taba, various options were explored to give the Palestinians more of a presence in East Jerusalem, which they claim as their capital. The peripheral villages and neighborhoods to the north and south of the city might have been ceded, although the Palestinians might have received less than full sovereignty over them—for example, "functional autonomy," "administrative control," or "limited sovereignty." In Taba, Israel considered ceding some parts of the core areas as well: some of the "Holy Basin" between the Old City and the Mount of Olives, downtown East Jerusalem, the Sheikh Jarrah Quarter, and the Muslim and Christian Quarters in the Old City. The Temple Mount/Haram al-Sharif issue remained unresolved, with Israel prepared to cede "functional sovereignty" (though not official) to the upper area of the mosques, while retaining sole sovereignty over the lower Western Wall.

Regardless of the size of the territorial compromises, Israel will not cede the entire area of East Jerusalem, where about 200,000 Israelis now outnumber Palestinians. Since the settlements there were situated strategically for maximum control of territory and movement, and since they are today in the process of being connected, any Palestinian patches would have only tenuous connections to each other and to the proposed Palestinian capital in Abu Dis. The Palestinian presence in Jerusalem would be fragmented and barely viable as an urban and economic center. Moreover, it would be entirely surrounded by the outer ring of Israeli Greater Jerusalem, hemming it in and preventing Palestinian East Jerusalem's normal urban and economic development. (Indeed, functionally ceding Palestinian areas of East Jerusalem to the Palestinians—relinquishing an unwanted population of some 200,000 people without relinquishing control—while incorporating the surrounding settlements into a Greater Jerusalem, would increase the majority of Jews in the expanded city from the present 70 percent to 85 percent.)

Israeli Control over Highways and Movement

Over the past decades (and especially during the Oslo peace process), Israel has been constructing a system of major highways and bypass roads designed to link its settlements, to create barriers between Palestinian areas and to incorporate the West Bank into Israel proper. Even if physical control over the highways is relinquished, strategic parts will remain under Israeli control, including the Eastern Ring Road, the Jerusalem–Etzion Bloc highway, Road 45 from Tel Aviv to Ma'ale Adumim, a section of Highway 60 from Jerusalem to Beit El and Ofra, and the western portion of the Trans-Samaria highway leading to the Ariel Bloc. In terms of the movement of people and goods, this will effectively divide the Palestinian entity into at least four cantons: the northern West Bank, the southern West Bank, East Jerusalem and Gaza. There are other restrictions as well. The "safe passages" from Gaza to the West Bank, crucial to the viability of a Palestinian state, will only be administered by the Palestinians; they will not receive extra-territorial status. And Israel insists on retaining rights of "emergency deployment" both to the highway system and to the Jordan Valley, severely compromising Palestinian sovereignty. Indeed, the highways would retain the status of Israeli "security roads," meaning that Palestinian development along them would remain limited.

To fully understand the role of the highway grid in completing the process of incorporation, one must link these West Bank developments to the ambitious Trans-Israel Highway project. Already in 1977, in his master plan for the settlement and incorporation of the West Bank, Ariel Sharon presented his "Seven Stars" plan calling for contiguous Israeli urban growth straddling both sides of the Green Line. The Trans-Israel Highway, which hugs the border of the West Bank, will provide a new "central spine" to the country. Hundreds of thousands of Israelis will be resettled in the many towns and cities planned along the length of the highway, especially along the Green Line and in areas of the Galilee now heavily populated by Arabs. New and expanded Israeli cities, towns and settlements on both sides of the Green Line will form a new metropolitan core region in which Metropolitan Tel Aviv (including the Modi'in area settlements, Rosh Ha-ayin and the Ariel bloc) meets Metropolitan Jerusalem (stretching from Modi'in, Kiryat Sefer, Beit Shemesh and the Etzion Bloc across the most of the central West Bank to the settlements east of Ma'ale Adumim). The Trans-Israel Highway, articulating as it does with the highways and settlement blocs of the West Bank, will move the population center of Israel eastward, reconfiguring the entire country.

An Answer to Israeli Security Concerns

"Security" is defined by Israel in such maximalist terms that it ensures Israeli political, military, and economic control. Israel insists that a Palestinian state must be demilitarized and forbidden to enter into military pacts with other states, that Israel control Palestinian airspace, and that it reserve the right to deploy forces in the Jordan Valley in the indeterminate event that it perceives a threat of invasion. Controlling Palestinian labor and commercial movement through the imposition of security borders, part of Israel's declared policy of "separation" from the Palestinians, constitutes additional constraints on Palestinian development, dividing the less than 20 percent of Palestine that would be the Palestinian state from the more than 80 percent that is Israel.

Limited Palestinian Sovereignty

A Palestinian state would possess limited sovereignty only. It would be demilitarized and unable to form military alliances not approved by Israel. It would have jurisdiction over its borders, but would have certain restrictions as to who may enter (especially vis-à-vis the refugee issue). And restrictions regarding military contingencies (defined by Israel) would apply.

For all their shortcomings, the Taba negotiations demonstrated that a path to peace exists. After seven years of fruitless negotiations, the essential issues of the conflict were finally defined and even discussed in some detail. Sa'eb Erekat, a senior Palestinian negotiator, claimed that in another two weeks the sides would have achieved a mutually acceptable agreement. But the talks were broken off by Barak. They came too late in the process. Just before his decisive defeat by Sharon in February 2001, Barak declared all the tentative agreements reached at Taba "null and void." Since then he has repeatedly said that Israel should not relinquish more than 85 percent of the occupied territories.

Despite the impression made in Camp David and Taba that Israel was forthcoming and that Palestinian "intransigence" prevented the sides from reaching agreement, the truth is that after seven years of negotiations Israel refused to dismantle its occupation. While territory was offered, the matrix of control remained intact and prevented the emergence of a viable and truly sovereign Palestinian state. No one who followed Israel's relentless expansion of its occupation on the ground would have detected the slightest hint that Israel had ever even contemplated a viable Palestinian state. In fact, Israel's activities on the ground completely prejudiced the outcome of the negotiations. During the years of negotiations between 1993 and 2000 Israel:

- turned what was to be a transitory arrangement for the orderly handing over of authority to the Palestinians—Areas A, B, and C—into a permanent system of dismemberment and control;
- expropriated 200 square kilometers of farm and pasture land from its Palestinian owners for exclusively Israeli settlements and roads;
- uprooted some 80,000 olive and fruit trees to permit Israeli construction and to deny ownership to Palestinian landowners (more than 100,000 fruit trees have since been uprooted in the course of suppressing the second intifada);
- established thirty new settlements, including whole cities like Kiryat

Sefer and Tel Zion, and constructed 90,000 new housing units in East Jerusalem and the settlements;
- demolished more than 1,200 Palestinian homes;
- doubled its settler population;
- constructed 250 miles of massive highways and bypass roads;
- imposed a permanent closure over the occupied territories;
- exploited the Palestinians' natural resources, especially water;
- vandalized the West Bank and parts of Jerusalem, destroying its historical landscape and turning it into a waste-disposal site;
- inaugurated plans for "unilateral separation" that include fencing off Palestinian "self-rule pockets" from Israel by means of a massive system of bunkers, walls, minefields, security crossings, checkpoints, and other fortifications, all designed to protect those parts of the West Bank that "we want and need to defend."

Even after the collapse of the Camp David negotiations (which Clinton and Barak squarely blamed on Arafat), Palestinians feared that Israel and the United States would succeed in pressuring Arafat to sign on to Israel's "take it or leave it" offer. (In the three months following Camp David the sides met fifty-two times.) Faced with the prospect of being locked forever into a tiny, non-viable bantustan, the Palestinian street rose up in its second intifada. Although Sharon's visit to the Haram al-Sharif/Temple Mount and the violent response of the Israeli police to nonviolent Palestinian protests triggered the uprising, it was directed as much at Arafat as against the occupation. The street's central message to Arafat was: "Do not sign the Camp David agreement." The intifada spelled the final rejection by the Palestinian people of the Oslo process, which they considered a sophisticated form of apartheid. Since then the intifada has turned into a full-scale war for independence.

DISMANTLING THE MATRIX OF CONTROL: THE ONLY WAY OUT

Despite the fierce military attacks waged upon them and the relentless campaign of attrition, the Palestinians are holding out for a linkage between an end to the violence and a political process. An end to their resistance without such a linkage—which the United States and Israel are urging upon them—would be counterproductive. If anything it would only perpetuate the occupation, removing any motivation Israel might have to address Palestinian claims and giving America the "industrial quiet" it so fervently seeks. And a return to negotiations is also meaningless if the dead-end process of Oslo is not to be repeated. If renewed negotiations are to succeed, they must include the following elements missing from Oslo:

- *An explicit declaration of the eventual goals of the negotiations.* These are a viable and truly sovereign Palestinian state, together with an Israel enjoying security and regional integration (a position very close to the Saudi plan).
- *A direct connection between the negotiations and the realities on the ground.* Oslo was formulated in a way that put off the "hard issues" (read: the issues most crucial to the Palestinians) until the final stages of the negotiations. Jerusalem, borders, water, settlements, the fate of the refugees, and security arrangements—all these issues (except the last, important mainly to Israel) were put off during the seven years of negotiations. Although Article IV of the 1993 Declaration of Principles talks about preserving the "integrity" of the West Bank and Gaza during negotiations, it did not prevent Israel from creating facts on the ground, which, as we have seen, completely prejudiced the discussions.
- *Reference to international law and human rights.* In Oslo, almost every protection and source of leverage the Palestinians possessed—including the Geneva Conventions and most UN resolutions—were set aside in favor of bilateral power negotiations in which Israel had a tremendous advantage. Virtually all the elements of the occupation comprising the matrix of control stand in violation of international law. The Fourth Geneva Convention in particular, signed and ratified by Israel, protects civilians living under occupation. Because it defines occupation as a temporary situation that will eventually be resolved through negotiations, it prohibits occupying powers from making their presence permanent—precisely what the matrix of control is intended to do.

If the Palestinians are to be held accountable for their terrorist actions, then Israel must be held accountable for policies and acts of state terrorism (for example, attacks on densely populated civilian centers with F-16s and Apache gunships, disproportionate violence against civilian populations, collective punishment, assassinations, and the indiscriminate use of snipers). Israel must also be held accountable for the structural violence inherent in its occupation (house demolitions, land expropriation, settlements, destruction of agricultural land, monopolization of water supplies, impoverishment through economic closure, induced emigration, and all the other expressions of occupation). Like other human rights covenants, the Fourth Geneva Convention holds accountable individuals who have committed "grave breaches" of the Convention (Article 146). Yet, with the help of its own legal system and the connivance of the international community, Israel acts with absolute impunity vis-à-vis international law, and has thus far escaped accountability.

In short, only negotiations based on international law—as well as UN resolutions—will give the Palestinians the instruments necessary to dismantle the occupation. Unless the issues of control, viability and sovereignty become formal elements in the negotiations, a non-viable and dependent Palestinian mini-state will be the result. An understanding of the matrix of control is essential for comprehending the sources of the present conflict, suggesting effective ways to end the occupation and ensuring that negotiations conclude with a just peace that is in everyone's interest.

Some 70 percent of the Palestinian people are refugees. No resolution of the conflict is possible without addressing their rights, needs and grievances. Israel must acknowledge its active role in creating the refugee problem and recognize the refugees' right of return. The Palestinians, and the wider Arab world that endorsed the Saudi plan, have indicated their willingness, once that is done, to negotiate a mutually agreed-upon actualization of that right based on settlement in the Palestinian state, compensation for those wishing to remain where they are and resettlement in other countries, as well as the return of a certain number of refugees to Israel itself.

For many reasons—political, ideological and emotional—peace will not come from Israel, and the Palestinians cannot shake off the occupation by themselves. It is up to the governments of the world to foster a just peace. Yet, because the governments have been remiss in their responsibility, it is up to us, the international civil society of NGOs, faith-based organizations, political groups, human rights advocates and just plain world citizens, to ensure that such a process begin. April 9, the day the Jenin refugee camp fell to Israeli forces, was called by the Israeli newspaper *Kol Ha'ir* "the first day of apartheid." This is the historical moment in which our effectiveness, our very relevance, will be tested. Having shed the naïvete of Oslo, we must follow the upcoming political process with eyes wide-open and critical. Our goal must be to see a viable, sovereign state emerge in all the occupied territories (giving the Palestinians the right to negotiate border adjustments and other compromises as they see fit). Unlike Oslo, the political process must have a just peace—a viable Palestinian state and a just resolution of the refugee issue, as well as Israel's security concerns—as its explicit goal. And it must have a binding timetable.

As Israelis learned from the terrorist attack on the bus in Haifa the day after their "victory" in Jenin and Nablus, there is no military solution to the conflict. It is time to end the occupation and bring justice, peace, security and prosperity to everyone in the Middle East.

May 2002

4

POLITICUS INTERRUPTUS

Uri Avnery

LAST WEEK, IN Europe, I happened to pass a frozen lake. I was told that a few days before, it was possible to skate on it. But the temperature had risen and the ice cover had started to melt. It still covers the whole lake, but in many places it can be broken with a stick. I was warned not to try to stand on it, because it might break, and I would fall into the lake and disappear. But in a few days or weeks, I was promised, the ice would disappear and the beautiful lake would come to life again.

The situation in our country resembles this lake. The ice still covers the whole state, but it has started to melt. The ice is the Big Lie told by Ehud Barak and his companions. This lie is starting to break. Soon nothing will be left of it.

When the bunch of bankrupt politicians returned from Camp David, they fabricated the legend, which has since become a holy truth, as if given by God at Mount Sinai. Like the Ten Commandments of Moses, there are Eight Facts of Barak: I have turned every stone on the way to peace; I have submitted offers unprecedented in their generosity; I went further than any prime minister before me; I have given the Palestinians everything they wanted; Arafat has rejected all the offers; Arafat does not want peace; the Palestinians want to throw us into the sea; we have no partner for peace.

If Benjamin Netanyahu had said this, it would not have had any impact. Everybody knows that Netanyahu is a crook. If Sharon had said it, he would not have been believed, because everybody knows that Sharon is a Man of Blood, unable to distinguish between truth and untruth. But when it came from the leaders of the Labor Party, those eminent spokesmen for peace, it caused the collapse of the established peace movement.

Since then, many testimonies about Camp David have been published, including some by pro-Israeli American eyewitnesses. All of them show that Barak's proposals fell far short of the essential minimum for peace: end the occupation, establish a Palestinian state side by side with Israel, give up all the occupied territories (all in all, 22 percent of Palestine under the British Mandate), return to the Green Line (with the possibility of mutually agreed swaps of territories), turn East Jerusalem into the capital of Palestine, return the settlers and soldiers to Israel, and end the tragedy of the refugees without damage to Israel.

When the Big Lie exploded, an alternative lie was put out: Some months after the Camp David talks were renewed in Taba in January 2001, Barak's men made offers unprecedented in their generosity, gave the Palestinians everything, but *Arafat refused to sign,* which shows that he does not want peace, etc.

Now Miguel Angel Moratinos, the European Union emissary for peace in the Middle East, has come along and buried this lie, too. The Spanish diplomat, who was in Taba but did not take part in the talks, has published a long and detailed report about what really happened there.

The clear conclusion is that at Taba the sides indeed came dramatically closer to each other. Gaps remained between their positions in almost all areas, but they were quantitative rather than qualitative gaps. Clearly, if the talks had gone on for another few days or weeks, a historic agreement would have been achieved.

So what happened? Is it true that Arafat refused to sign? Not at all. Arafat did not refuse to sign. He wanted to continue the negotiations until there was an agreement to sign.

It was not Arafat who broke off the talks at this critical moment, when the light at the end of the tunnel was clearly visible to the negotiators, but Barak. He ordered his men to break off and return home. Why?

The Taba talks began after the outbreak of the second intifada. After Sharon's September 28, 2000, invasion of the Temple Mount with Barak's permission, and after seven Arab protesters were shot by Internal Security Minister Shlomo Ben-Ami's police, bloody incidents occurred daily. The Taba talks were held "under fire"—a process that is quite normal in history. After all, negotiations are held in order to put an end to the fire.

On that day, two Israelis were murdered in a Palestinian town. The Palestinians said that this was revenge for the murder of a local leader. But it was enough for Barak to break off the talks.

What was the real reason? The answer must be found in the mind of Barak. After all, it happened to Barak time and again: Whenever he got close to an agreement, he withdrew at the last moment.

It started at the very beginning of his term of office. As will be recalled, he wanted to come to an agreement with the Syrians first, in order to isolate the Palestinians. Complete agreement was almost reached, when suddenly everything broke down. Assad wanted Syrian territory to extend to the shores of the Sea of Galilee, while Barak wanted the border to be a hundred meters away from the shore. Because of the hundred meters, Barak rejected the historic agreement that was at hand. (These days, comics say that Barak should have fixed the border at the shoreline as it was then, as the sea has retreated many hundreds of meters since then.)

The same happened at Camp David. Agreement was possible. All the participants believed at the time that it was already close. Then something happened to Barak. As the Israeli participants testify, Barak simply freaked out. He cut himself off, did not shave and refused to meet even with his closest assistants.

Something similar happened at Taba. When the agreement was at hand, Barak ordered the talks to be broken off. The actual pretext does not matter.

When something like that occurs again and again, it raises questions. It may be called "politicus interruptus." A moment before the consummation, Barak draws back. I am not a psychiatrist and am not qualified to deal with mental problems. But I believe that every time, when Barak saw the actual price of peace in front of him, he shrunk back at the last moment. There was a dissonance between the price of peace (withdrawal from the occupied territories, evacuation of settlements, conceding East Jerusalem and the Temple Mount, return of a symbolic number of refugees) and the ideas he was brought up on. He could not shoulder the responsibility and broke down. At the same time, he expanded the settlements at a frantic pace.

Adding sin to crime (as the Hebrew expression goes), he covered his personal collapse with the Big Lie, which caused a national collapse.

Now the lie is starting to break up. The open discussion of war crimes, the declaration of hundreds of soldiers that they refuse to serve in the Palestinian territories, the call of the reserve generals for an end to the occupation, the new voices in the media, the call of courageous artists, the big demonstration of twenty-seven militant peace organizations (including Gush Shalom), the following big Peace Now demonstration—all these show that the ice is starting to melt.

This is only the beginning. Now is the time for all those who were waiting to join the effort. As Churchill said after the Allied victory in Egypt: "This is not the end. It is not even the beginning of the end. But it is, perhaps, the end of the beginning."

February 23, 2002

5

A BETRAYAL OF HISTORY

Avi Shlaim

IN A FEBRUARY 21, 2002 article in the Guardian, *Israeli historian Benny Morris announced that his thinking about the Israeli-Palestinian conflict had "radically changed." No longer "cautiously optimistic" that a resolution would be found, Morris now believed that Arafat had in 2000 rejected "a reasonable peace agreement," and "instead of continuing to negotiate, the Palestinians . . . launched the intifada." Despairing of a near-term solution, Morris now believed that "the Palestinians, at least in this generation, do not intend peace. . . . They want all of Palestine." This response by Avi Shlaim appeared the next day.*

"A nation," wrote the French philosopher Ernest Renan, "is a group of people united by a mistaken view about the past and a hatred of their neighbors." By this definition, Benny Morris may now be counted as a true member of the Israeli nation. In his account of his "conversion," Benny explains that, although he has not undergone a brain transplant as far as he can remember, his thinking about the current Middle East crisis and its protagonists has radically changed during the past two years.

Willingness to re-examine one's thinking is always a commendable trait in a historian. Unfortunately, in Benny's case the re-examination is confined to only one protagonist in the Middle East conflict: the Palestinians. As a consequence, his new version of the recent history of the conflict has more in common with propaganda than with genuine history. Like most nationalist versions of history, it is simplistic, selective and self-serving.

By his own account, Benny's conversion was a pretty dramatic affair. He imagines that he feels a bit like those Western fellow travelers rudely awakened by the trundle of Russian tanks crashing into Budapest in 1956. But there is surely some mistake in this analogy. Benny could not possibly have heard the trundle of Palestinian tanks crashing into any Israeli city, because there are no Palestinian tanks. What he might have heard is the sound of Merkava tanks invading Palestinian cities on the West Bank and refugee camps in Gaza in the most flagrant violation of a long series of agreements that placed these areas under the control of the Palestinian Authority. Another minor flaw in Benny's analogy is that the Palestinians, by any reckoning, can only be seen as the victims, while Israel is the aggressive and overbearing military superpower. If we are going to look for historical antecedents for this grossly unequal contest, it would make more sense to update the biblical image of David and Goliath: a Palestinian David facing an Israeli Goliath.

There is a historical irony in Benny's conversion to the orthodox Zionist rendition of the past, for he was one of the trailblazers of the "new history," which placed Israel's political and military conduct under an uncompromising lens. Indeed, it was he who coined the term "the new historiography" in order to distinguish it from the traditional pro-Zionist literature about the birth of Israel and the first Arab-Israeli war of which he was so savagely critical.

His 1988 book, *The Birth of the Palestinian Refugee Problem, 1947– 1949*, drove a coach and horses through the claim that the Palestinians left Palestine of their own accord or on orders from their leaders. With a great wealth of recently declassified material, he analyzed the role that Israel played in precipitating the Palestinian exodus. Three or four subsequent books consolidated Benny's reputation as the standard-bearer of the new historiography. The hallmark of his approach was to stick as closely as possible to the documentary evidence, to record rather than to evaluate. While his findings were original and arresting, he upheld the highest standards of historical scholarship, and he wrote with almost clinical detachment.

Sadly, the article in the *Guardian* does not display any of Benny's former scholarly objectivity or rigorous use of evidence. Instead of evidence we are treated to a rambling and self-pitying monologue, seething with contempt and hatred for the Arabs in general and the Palestinians in particular.

The message, pithily summed up in a long interview that Benny gave to *Yediot Ahronot* about his highly publicized conversion, is that "the Arabs are responsible." Where no evidence is available to sustain the argument of Arab intransigence, Benny makes it up by drawing on his fertile imagination.

According to Benny, what stayed the hand of Hafez Assad of Syria, and that of his son and successor Bashar, from signing a peace treaty was not quibbles over a few hundred yards but a basic refusal to make peace with the Jewish state. The evidence? Benny can see the father, on his deathbed, telling his son: "Whatever you do, don't make peace with the Jews; like the Crusaders, they too will vanish." It would appear that Benny can no longer tell the difference between genuine history and fiction or fabrication along the lines of *The Protocols of the Elders of Zion*. At this rate Benny is in danger of becoming what Isaiah Berlin once described as "a very rare thing—a genuine charlatan."

Most of Benny's venom and vitriol are, however, reserved for the Palestinians in what amounts to a remarkable attempt to blame the victims for their own misfortunes. He trots out again Abba Eban's tired old quip that the Palestinians "have never missed an opportunity to miss an opportunity," blithely disregarding all the opportunities for peace that Israel has missed since 1967. But the main reason, we are told, around which Benny's pessimism gathered and crystallized was the figure of Yasser Arafat, the leader of the Palestinian movement since the late 1960s. Arafat-bashing has become a national sport in Israel of late, and Benny has a field day, calling him, among other things, an "implacable nationalist and inveterate liar." To be sure, Arafat is no paragon of virtue, but it is far too easy and too simplistic to place the entire blame for the failure of the Oslo peace process on the shoulders of one individual.

Like Benny, I was cautiously optimistic after Israel and the Palestine Liberation Organization signed the Oslo accord in September 1993, but our interpretation of the subsequent history is very different. Oslo represented a historic compromise for the Palestinians: They gave up their claim to 78 percent of Mandatory Palestine in return for a state of their own over the remaining 22 percent, comprising the West Bank and Gaza. Israel, for its part, recognized the PLO as the legitimate representative of the Palestinian people, and the two sides agreed to resolve their outstanding differences by peaceful means.

For Benny the principal reason for the collapse of this historic compromise is Palestinian mendacity; for me it is Israeli expansionism. The building of settlements in the occupied territories has always been illegal under international law and an obstacle to peace. Expanding Jewish settlements on the West Bank is not a violation of the letter of the Oslo accord, but it is most certainly a violation of its spirit. Israel's protests of peaceful intentions were vitiated by its policy of expropriating more and more Palestinian land and building more Jewish settlements on this land. By continuing to build settlements, Israel basically went back on its side of the deal that had been concluded at Oslo.

The main landmarks in the breakdown of the Oslo peace process are the Camp David summit of July 2000 and the outbreak of the intifada toward the end of September of that year. Israel's official history is full of myths, as Benny knows so well from the earlier stage in his career, when he was in the business of exploding national myths and slaughtering sacred cows. The latest national myth is that of the generous offer that Ehud Barak is said to have made to Arafat at Camp David, only to be confronted with a flat rejection and a return to violence. There is a broad national consensus behind this myth, including the left and the peace camp, but popular support is not the same as evidence.

The role of the historian is to subject the claims of the protagonists to critical scrutiny in the light of all the available evidence. In this instance, however, Benny seems to have swallowed the official Israeli line on Camp David hook, line and sinker. The firsthand account of the American official Robert Malley is not even mentioned.* It suggests that Barak mishandled the summit from start to finish. Benny also

---

* "Camp David: The Tragedy of Errors," Robert Malley and Hussein Agha, *The New York Review of Books*, August 9, 2001.

glosses over the fact that the al-Aqsa intifada, which has so far claimed the lives of 941 Palestinians and 273 Israelis,* broke out not on orders from Arafat but in response to a provocative visit to the Haram al-Sharif by the then-leader of the opposition, Ariel Sharon.

Benny's account of the next phase in the "final status" negotiations is hopelessly inaccurate. On December 23, 2000, President Bill Clinton presented his "parameters" for a final settlement of the conflict. These parameters reflected the long distance he had traveled from the American bridging proposals tabled at Camp David toward meeting Palestinian aspirations. The new plan provided for an independent Palestinian state over the whole of Gaza and 94–96 percent of the West Bank (with some territorial compensation from Israel proper); Palestinian sovereignty over the Arab parts of Jerusalem, Israeli sovereignty over the Jewish parts; and a solution to the Palestinian refugee problem in which the new state would be the focal point for the refugees who choose to return to the area.

According to Benny, the Palestinian leadership rejected "the Barak-Clinton peace proposals of July-December 2000." In fact, they rejected Barak's proposals of July and accepted in principle Clinton's proposals of December, as did the Israeli leadership. Both sides had their reservations. On Jerusalem, the Israeli reservations were more substantial than the Palestinian ones. Benny not only conflates two entirely separate sets of proposals; he makes no mention at all of the negotiations at Taba in the last week of January 2001.

At Taba the two teams made considerable progress on the basis of the Clinton parameters and came closer to an overall agreement than at any other time in the history of this conflict. But by this time, Clinton and Barak were on their way out and Sharon was on his way in. During the run-up to the elections, Barak hardened his line on Jerusalem. At this critical juncture, as so often in the past, the peace process was held hostage to internal Israeli politics. With Sharon's election, all the progress made at Taba toward a "final status" agreement was rendered

* According to B'Tselem, the Israeli Information Center for Human Rights in the Occupied Territories, more than 1,400 Palestinians and 469 Israelis have been killed as of the end of May 2002.

null and void. A new and grisly chapter in the history of the conflict was about to begin.

Benny's conclusion follows naturally from his deficient and defective account of the history of the last decade, and especially of the last two years. His conclusion is that the root problem today is the Palestinian leadership's denial of the legitimacy of the Jewish state. The conclusion that I draw from my version of history is that the root problem today is the Jewish state's continuing occupation of most of the Palestinian territories that it captured in June 1967.

All the neighboring Arab states, as well as the Palestinians, recognize Israel's right to exist within its pre-1967 borders. None of them recognizes the legitimacy of the Jewish colonial project beyond the Green Line. Nor do I. This is where Benny Morris and I part company. His post-conversion interpretation of history is old history with a vengeance. It is indistinguishable from the propaganda of the victors. He used to have the courage of his convictions. He now has the courage of his prejudices.

February 22, 2002

6

A TIME OF OCCUPATION

Adi Ophir

THE WRITINGS ASSEMBLED here are being published during a time of occupation. As a result of the Palestinian armed struggle against the Israeli occupation, the occupation is now the overt, official state of affairs, and can no longer be denied by anyone. Despite the simulation of a "peace process," despite the doctrinal vagueness, despite the hybrid situations, the mixed areas and the open borders, the conditions are clearer today than they have ever been: Reconciliation between Jews and Palestinians will occur only if and when the occupation ends, in the fullest sense of the word. The occupation is defined according to the borders determined in the cease-fire agreement at the end of the 1948 war. All Jewish settlements established after the war of 1967, including all neighborhoods in and around Jerusalem, stultify the ability to end the occupation. In order to attain reconciliation, Israel will have to evacuate the vast majority of these settlements, including Palestinian Jerusalem. The Jews will not be able to both maintain sovereignty in Jerusalem and appease the Palestinians and, by extension, the entire Arab world. Settlements remaining under Israeli sovereignty—including Jewish neighborhoods in parts of Jerusalem beyond the 1967 borders—can remain only upon Palestinian agreement, as part of their concession for an accord and in return for fair Israeli concessions; the

Translated by Jessica Cohen

formula must assure a reciprocity of concessions. These are the terms. This is the truth. Everything else is lies, facades, disguises, deceit. This is an essential point of departure for any serious discussion of a solution to the Israeli-Palestinian struggle.

These are the terms under the current conditions. These are the terms when one accepts, if indeed one does—out of *realpolitik* considerations—that the Jewish and Palestinian societies are currently controlled by a nationalistic agenda and do not comprise significant forces actively opposing the subjugation of any political settlement to nation-state principles. But even under these historical conditions, these are not the *only* terms for an agreement. It is now clear that ending the occupation, though an essential condition for achieving reconciliation between the two peoples, is not a sufficient one. The conflict between the Jews and the Palestinians did not begin with the 1967 occupation and will not be over when the occupation is abolished. Reconciliation will be reached only when there is a compromise that encompasses the 1948 refugees. This issue is also a prerequisite for any chance of reconciliation with the Palestinian citizens of Israel and of regularizing their status as equal citizens and members of a recognized national minority. Is such a compromise attainable today, in this generation? The answer is unclear. It is difficult at present to ascertain the earnestness of the Palestinian demand for complete implementation of the right of return as part of any agreement. It is equally difficult to guess what might be the limit of Israeli flexibility on this question, which most Israelis have preferred to repress until now. This is not one of the issues that has been clarified since the al-Aqsa intifada erupted. It is clear, however, that the question of the 1948 refugees can no longer be obscured. Without a compromise on the refugee problem, there will be no reconciliation and Israel will not emerge from under the shadow of apartheid. An Israeli refusal to either recognize the right of return *on principle,* or commence a *practical* debate over its partial and symbolic actualization, will perpetuate the processes, already in effect, of institutionalizing the binational reality of an apartheid regime. This is the inevitable result of a nationalistic agenda that has been imposed for years on a binational reality.

When the Oslo process collapsed at the end of summer 2000 and the intifada erupted, the Israeli public underwent a rapid shift to the right. Many perceived the failure of the Camp David talks and the subsequent violent outburst as a sign of the Palestinian pretense that had characterized the negotiations from the start, or of the Palestinian insistence on principles that endanger the very existence of the State of Israel—an insistence that proved, in retrospect, that there was never anyone to talk with in the first place. At the moment of truth, they claimed, the cat was let out of the bag. That was true, except that the cat was out, first and foremost, of the Israeli bag. The left that quickly slid to the right was a left that had never internalized the fact that the occupation is the point of departure; that ending the occupation is a condition of reconciliation—not vice versa. This large segment of the public, which soon became a partner in Sharon's right-wing government, never perceived the occupation as the template for the Jewish-Palestinian power relationship and social interactions in the territories. Moreover, they never grasped the extent to which the occupation also determines relationship patterns, both between Jews and Palestinians and among Jews within the Green Line, and shapes each side's perception of the other and interpretation of its acts and words. Only a very few on the radical left, who did not forget the state of occupation, who knew that diplomacy had long been detached from events in the occupied territories, who persisted in seeing the ongoing injustice, the suffering and the humiliation, were not surprised by the outburst of rage and violence of the intifada, nor by the force of the Israeli violence employed to suppress it. These are people whose critical faculties were not anesthetized by the Oslo process, whether or not they supported it. From the moment the productive role-playing facilitated by the Oslo process was over, the divide between two segments of the Israeli public was once again apparent: On the one side were the consistent opponents of the occupation, on the other were those willing, somewhat uneasily, to accept the continuation of the occupation, together with those attempting to perpetuate it by any means possible.

The fact that today only very few Jews remain on the one side, while the other encompasses the majority of Israeli Jews, should not mislead us: This is the true divide. Disagreements among the groups within

each of these two camps are negligible in comparison with this fundamental schism. This is what transpired at the moment of truth, the beginning of the new intifada, which shattered the fantasy of "the end of
the conflict" and "peace is around the corner." The collapse of the political course imposed by Barak under the auspices of Clinton, the widespread feeling that Israel had put the Palestinians to the test and they
had failed it—thus, in effect, betraying the entire peace camp, the violent Palestinian eruption—all these created a situation in which most
Israeli Jews were forced to expose the fundamental conceptual framework within which they perceive political reality. This contradictory
framework portrays the relationship between the two peoples as a supposedly symmetrical relationship between two national movements of
equal standing, at the same time accepting the occupation as a paradigm of asymmetrical power relations and ignoring its continuous
history. It dictates a willingness to make "concessions," alongside an im-
perious demand that the other side gratefully recognize the generous
handout. It represses the Palestinian tragedy and denies Israel's role in
creating and preserving it, while amplifying the loss and suffering on
the Israeli side. It blurs the true power relationship between the two
sides and ignores the magnitude of the Palestinian distress, just as it disproportionately accentuates the Palestinian threat to Israel. This incon-
gruous structure was, for most Israelis, a conceptual shelter into which
they retreated with alarm when the Palestinian uprising began, and by
means of which they interpreted the uprising and the direct sense of
menace it stirred in them. This was also the source of their justification
of the Israeli violence used to suppress it.

During moments of truth, the choice is sharp and clear. It forces a
decision that brings out the truth of one's stance and the meaning of
one's acts and intentions, a decision whose implications may be far-
reaching. It was the point in time and the particular circumstances that
invited such decisions. In the fall of 2000, a few key officials were compelled to make decisions that have since shaped the fate of the inhabitants of Israel-Palestine—indeed determined their very life and death,
and will continue to do so for many years. The Israeli leaders chose to
ignore the circumstances under which the Palestinian uprising broke

out, the daily anguish of the occupation and the frustration and hope-lessness that nurtured it, instead reacting to the uprising as if it were a threat to Israel's existence, using immense force completely dispropor-tionate to the actual threat. At the same time, the Palestinian leaders chose to ignore the Israeli sense of threat and did not take into account the Israeli readiness to employ full military force to suppress the upris-ing and preserve the occupation.

The Israeli response generated a chain reaction of violent escalation. Networks of "normal" interactions between Israelis and Palestinians were ripped apart, apparatus that were already working to coordinate in the various friction zones and mollify the violent reactions fell apart; reconciliation proponents on both sides either aligned themselves with the right wing or were squeezed into the extreme margins. Hatred and a thirst for vengeance were everywhere. The Palestinian decision to react to the collapse of the Camp David negotiations with violence and terror and the Israeli decision to control the uprising and terror with massive force created a whirlwind of violence that today threatens to obliterate not only the prospect of reconciliation between the two people and the Palestinians' chance of leading some semblance of a normal life, but also the hope of maintaining civil and democratic life in Israel itself. The Palestinians' choice of violence and terror results in endless suffer-ing with no real hope on the political horizon, the development of a regime of armed gangs, and the destruction of the fabric of civilian life. The implication of this choice on the Israeli side is an acceleration in the nationalization processes of the Jewish state and an institutionaliza-tion of its regime as one of apartheid.

This course of deterioration is the result of decisions made by few—Ehud Barak, Minister of Public Security Shlomo Ben-Ami, army Chief of Staff Shaul Mofaz, Yasser Arafat, secretary general of Fatah in the West Bank Marwan Barghouti, PA chief of Preventive Security in Gaza Mohammed Dahlan, the Hamas leaders. Following the acts of violence, both peoples aligned themselves with the right wing in response to "their" violence, and out of a need to justify "our" violence. The real de-cision engendered by this period, at least in Israel, was not made by a broad section of the population, nor was it reflected in the public sphere, the political arena, or the elections that brought Sharon to power. The Israeli majority that supports the government policy today was created in response to decisions made by a few figures whose realm of action was removed from any public or party debate.

From the collapse of the Camp David talks until Sharon was elected prime minister, Israel was in an interim state, a state of protracted decision making. Under these circumstances, the governmental systems disconnected from one another, each continuing to pursue its own separate course, almost with the inertia of a satellite that has strayed from its orbit around Earth. The army was gradually severed from the government. Senior army officers stopped taking part in determining political objectives and implementing them, and statesmen stopped participating in the shaping of military policy. While the ruling politicians talked of restraint, the generals rolled out the tanks, launched rockets and sent snipers to kill in the Palestinian Authority areas. When the former spoke favorably of a possible settlement, the latter condemned it. When the right wing opposition politicians called on the IDF to prevail, the generals told them the IDF was incapable of doing so, certainly not on its own. And all this time, fragments of diplomatic negotiations proceeded, covertly and overtly, oblivious to the political crises, detached from the number of casualties, from the closures and the encirclements and the elimination lists. (How can they have the impudence to negotiate while there are shootings, the opposition cried, ignoring the fact that this was exactly what the Palestinian leadership had been doing all along when it negotiated under the shadow of the occupation violence, which never let up for a moment.) The field was covered in blood, while senior officials flitted from one country to another in Europe, Africa, and America, from one capital to the next, rushing to urgent meetings in grand palaces and closed military bases, with or without notifying the press. Maps were spread out, stages were proposed, papers passed from hand to hand. But papers were dismissed as "non-papers," maps did not map, understandings were denied and no agreement materialized.

If an agreement had been reached during the final days of Barak's government, or if the negotiations—at least in the Oslo format—had been declared completely terminated, the aberrant satellites would have reconvened on one peripheral course. The government would once again have needed both the Knesset and the army, the army would once again have operated according to the dictates of policy, and the diplomats would have gone on to reap the fruits or gather the shards, depending on the results. Both implementing a peace accord—the best-case scenario—and reinstituting and reorganizing the government of occupation and apartheid would have necessitated a reconvening of the state apparatus, a recalibration between the practices of aggression and the practices of ideology, between the methods of enforcing power and the methods of representing it.

This type of reconvening and recalibration would have claimed a high social price—a price that would certainly have been claimed even if an agreement were reached and ratified in an election. The government would then have had to rely on the majority that supported the agreement, including its Arab component, and would have been frequently forced to resort to its array of violent mechanisms to suppress Jewish terror and defeat Jewish civil disobedience. There may also have emerged a "rift in the nation." But the real problem facing supporters of the accord in this scenario would not have been the "rift in the nation," but rather the need to defeat the fear spread by talk of such a rift. An agreement could only have been reached at the cost of a publicized display of "a rift in the nation" and forceful suppression of the fragments that would have chosen violent opposition to the decision of the majority; this would have been a worthy price to pay. Had the peace camp managed to cause such a rift in the nation even without an agreement, even before Palestinian resistance forced Israel into a serious discussion of an agreement, even before such an agreement was on the horizon; had the left managed to cleave a rift because of the occupation and not because of the agreement, it would certainly have increased the chances of achieving such an agreement. Had the peace camp torn itself away from the segment of Israeli society that maintains the occupation in its acts, its way of life, its person and property, an agreement might have been reached years ago, lives might have been saved, some of the destruction and ruination might have been prevented. Openness, generosity, expressions of fraternity toward the right wing in its time of grief and sorrow—yes. A true concern for the safety and well-being of the settlers who would have to pay a hefty personal price at the time of evacuation—certainly. The conditions for all this, however, would be a new political partnership and the end of the occupation. Until then— the left should have said—let there be a rift in the nation.

But the left did not say this and no agreement was reached and there was no rift in the nation. Quite the opposite. The left glided to the right, the agreement papers were scattered in the wind and the nation re- united around the campfires of war. The 2001 pre-election period of protraction was replaced with a new kind of protraction—the protrac- tion that precedes an explosion. The implication of the election was that at least one decision had been made: At this stage there is no progress toward an agreement. The departure from the peace talks and the absence of any political program enabled a reconvening and recali- bration of the state mechanisms. The Israeli political system reverted to its "natural state" of the pre-Oslo years, a state of occupation, with one fundamental difference: The occupation had now become the legal, de- clared position of the Israeli government.

Even before the elections, some Israelis who saw themselves as left- ists spoke and wrote of a new civic agenda under these circumstances and accepted the need to protect the prospect of an Israeli civil society within the Green Line. These Israelis wished to quickly forget about the occupation. After all, this was how they had led their lives before the first intifada and this was how they had lived after the Oslo accords until the second intifada began. In one respect they were right: One cannot lead a proper civic life when the political system has become a regime of occupation. So they began, even before the elections, to talk of separa- tion. This talk was reinvigorated after the elections, particularly when it transpired that Sharon had no plan to negotiate a political solution. Only complete separation from the occupation can enable the condi- tions for the existence of a civil society; but under the current circum- stances, complete separation from the occupation is either a pipedream or pathological repression. Thence the awful logic of the deterioration since the Palestinians realized there was no longer a political horizon for their struggle against the occupation. The Palestinians increased the violence in order to remind the Israelis of the occupation, and the Israelis who had despaired of an agreement and wanted to repress the occupation quickly learned to ignore the intensity of the violence employed by the Israeli government to suppress Palestinian resistance. Some of the disconnected systems, particularly the government, the army, and the media, resumed their nurturing of each other and attempted to heal the rifts that threatened civil calm on the one side of the Green Line, destroyed the resistance and terror on the other side, and painted everything over with the colors of blood and earth—the colors of a persecuted nation, a nation with no choice. Thus the situation spiraled downward toward the next point of collapse.

In the mid 1990s, the Oslo accords created and institutionalized a disparity between the *de facto* situation in the territories—occupation, and the *de jure* situation—the peace process and partial agreements in preparation for the end of the occupation. Many people expressed doubts about the viability of this disparity, but only those with utterly deterministic minds would deny that it did embody a chance, if only a small one, that the *de facto* situation would also gradually be changed. Most of the Israeli public, however, including many moderates, did not understand the significance of the growing disparity between the *de facto* situation and the *de jure* representation for the Palestinians. The Israelis did not grasp the intensity of the expectations the agreement had engendered on the other side, nor the intensity of the frustration as the decolonization process ground to a halt and most of the occupation regime's apparatus continued to operate even after the majority of the Gaza Strip and many West Bank cities had been vacated by the Israeli army and handed over to the Palestinian Authority. Then came Barak, who renounced the gradation principle of the Oslo accords. He wanted peace now. He wanted everything, immediately. He broke the rules of the game, which had enabled the existence of a shred of a chance for progress. In the summer of 2000, when the peace talks at Camp David fell apart, the match was over. Gradually, with vigorous assistance from the intifada, all the playing courts were closed, and in February 2001 they sent the whole team home. Sharon's election and all his actions since have had one determinate meaning: There is no longer a disparity between the *de jure* state and the *de facto* state. The actual state of occupation is also the state on paper, both legally and formally. There is no political horizon, no process, no negotiations, no nothing. Only occupation.

Still, one important element remains from the Oslo process and the two intifadas (the one that gave birth to the peace process and the one that buried it): an acknowledgment of the occupation's temporariness. No one can seriously talk of perpetuating the occupation any longer, at least not in the form it has assumed since 1967. The temporariness of the occupation is both the *de jure* state and the *de facto* state. The temporariness itself has acquired *de jure* status. Temporariness is the new law of the occupation, and the violent Palestinian resistance both enforces this law and pushes it into the light. Since it erupted, it is absolutely clear—even to those who did not previously understand—that everything is temporary. But this temporariness has a terrible price in Israeli reactions: temporary takeover of Area A, temporary withdrawal from Area A, temporary encirclement and temporary closures, temporary transit permits, temporary revocation of permits, temporary enforcement of an elimination policy, temporary change in the open-fire orders, followed by yet another change. Only two things escape the grip of time and the squall of temporariness: the dead—forever—and the settlements—for now. When the occupier plays with time and temporariness like this, everything—everything that moves, everything that lives—becomes dependent on the arbitrariness of the occupier's decisions. The occupier is fully aware that he is always playing on borrowed time, in fact on stolen time, other people's time. This occupier is an unrestrained, almost boundless sovereign, because when everything is temporary almost anything—any crime, any form of violence—is acceptable, because the temporariness seemingly grants it a license, the license of the state of emergency. Whatever doesn't fly today, will fly tomorrow, when the Americans are busy with another war, when the Europeans look away to another corner of the world for a moment. Because whatever doesn't fly is prevented not by the sovereign being restrained by the power of the political system he leads, but rather by the

fact that he operates within the framework of international power rela-
tionships and depends upon the world power and its allies.

What choice do the occupied have in this state? Most Israeli Jews
think that because the Palestinians refused to accept the "generous
offer" they wished to impose on them, they should have waited pa-
tiently and continued talking indefinitely. But since February 2001, if
not earlier, the Palestinians have not had anyone to talk to or anything
to talk about, apart from cosmetic changes in the way they are being
dominated or an agreement to turn the occupation state back from
temporary to permanent. And the occupation continues, the violence
continues, the dispossession continues. What choice do the Palestinians
have? The liberal tradition of political thought in the West, the tradition
upon which the Israeli legal system is also based, and the mainstream
tradition of political action in the West—a tradition that Zionism,
which defines itself as the Jewish people's liberation movement, wished
to join—says that in such a situation the occupied have no choice: They
have no choice but to resist. As the poet Yitzhak Laor writes:

I have no
choice, even if everything is created by
the regime, even the history of
poetry, even the limits of
assertion, I have no choice
but to resist.*

The occupied party's resistance to the occupier is its moral right. Its
violent resistance to the occupation is a direct result of the violence of
the occupation itself. Such violent resistance is perhaps immoral and
perhaps unwise (under certain conditions it might be morally wrong
precisely *because* it is unwise). But according to the legal and political
tradition to which most of the political leadership in Israel belong,
there is no doubt that such resistance—or at least certain forms of it—
is legitimate. The Palestinians have no choice but to resist.

* Yitzhak Laor, *Layla bemalon zar* [A Night in a Foreign Hotel]. Tel Aviv: Kibbutz
Meuhad, 1992.

These simple statements can hardly be made out loud today. Only very few Israeli Jews are willing to openly state that they understand this resistance and support it, even if they cannot under any circumstances condone the criminal forms it sometimes assumes. The vast majority of Jewish Israelis are unable to admit today that the Palestinians have no choice. It is too threatening. It means that every Jewish victim was in vain. It undermines the mobilization efforts demanded by the new form of fighting, the new form of occupation. And so they claim that *they,* the Jews, have no choice. They turn the tables and portray themselves as once again fighting with their backs against the wall. This is the type of war they fight best, and so they would do well to present every war as if it were a "no alternative" war. They try to portray the Palestinian resistance in all its forms, from the most vile terror to the most heroic and respectable struggle, as a threat to the existence of the State of Israel and the entire Jewish people. In this state one must focus on the Jewish victims and look aside, systematically and deliberately, every time Palestinian victims come into sight. The daily victims of closures and encirclements are not even mentioned. The other victims are dismissed with military rhetoric: they are objects of "targeted eliminations" or subjects of "collateral damage." The blindness is systematic and contagious. Every day you find more and more people around you who have been affected by this blindness. The blinder one becomes, the greater one's fear, and thus the greater one's willingness to stand behind the threats embodied in the crimes. Israeli Jews must be blind in order to be able to accept the new form of the struggle with the Palestinians. They must be nationalistic so that they can live in peace with the war, the eliminations, the starvations and the curfews. Let us be clear—nationalism did not spawn the new form of occupation, but rather it was the new law of occupation, the unrestrained sovereign's law of temporariness, which caused nationalism to reemerge as state religion.

The Palestinian citizens of Israel were swept up in this process in October 2000. They also had no choice. How could they sit idly when their brothers were rising up and being killed? How can anyone not understand this? The disproportionately violent police response caused the death of thirteen citizens, some of whom were probably murdered in cold blood. Just like on the other side of the Green Line, here too the new form of violence necessitated a new form of justification. The Israeli Arabs were marked post-factum as a threat. In some cases this might turn out to be a self-fulfilling prophecy. Neither Jews nor Palestinians can reasonably discount the cases, few at this stage, of Israeli Palestinians who entered the armed conflict cycle and volunteered to commit acts of terror, including suicide terror. This terror fits perfectly into the new slot that has been allotted to the Israeli Arab—a return to the days of the "fifth column" and "the enemy within," a return to the days when it was possible to represent the Palestinian citizens of Israel as a threat to its existence.

An escalation in Jewish–Palestinian conflict within the Green Line is clearly in the interests of the right wing. It enables them to blur the difference between the Palestinians' civil struggle on the Israeli side of the Green Line and the liberation struggle of the Palestinians on the other side. Such escalation enables the creation of a public atmosphere that will tolerate the removal from the Knesset of leaders and parties who represent the Palestinian population in Israel, and the severe harm caused to the democratic representation of this sector. The removal of one leader or one party may cause a chain reaction within the Palestinian public in Israel which will ultimately result in the departure of this population from the entire election process. Without the Palestinian voters, the right wing's control of Israeli politics is assured for many years to come. They can even save on campaign financing.

Thus we see ideological motivations, whose essence is the need for nationalistic mobilization in order to justify the new form of the occupation regime, joining political motives, whose essence is the desire to see fewer Palestinians in the parliamentary arena. In any case, the result is a demonization of the political leadership of the Israeli Palestinian population and a delegalization of its civil struggle. For this reason it is important to the Jewish nationalists to point to the non-Jewish citizens' support of terror, which is allegedly intended to destroy the state of Israel. But the Palestinian citizens support the fight for national liberation, not terror. Terror is a pattern of action that contradicts the social-economic state, the emotional position, and the moral consciousness of the overwhelming majority of Palestinian Israeli citizens. The Israeli Palestinians' objection to the Israeli occupation, to fifty years of discrimination in a country willing to grant them deficient citizenship and unwilling to recognize them as a national sector, is a paradigm of civil objection. This is what the new Jewish nationalism finds hardest to swallow.

Hard to swallow not only because such civil resistance upsets the position arranged for the Arab in the new nationalistic ideology model, but because such civil resistance threatens the distorted conception of citizenship in the Jewish national state and the very ability to hide, in the long run, the basic contradiction between the Jewish element and the democratic element in the Jewish national state. Today, no one represents this threat better than Member of the Knesset Dr. Azmi Bishara. Bishara, a model citizen, an intellectual who could give civics lessons to most Members of the Knesset and school them in democracy, is today portrayed as a threat to the Israeli rule. A decisive majority of the Knesset House Committee supported lifting his parliamentary immunity and trying him for political speeches he delivered and assistance he gave to Israeli Palestinians to visit their relatives in Syria—acts that are an essential component of his function as a Member of the Knesset and of his loyalty to his constituents.* This majority expresses the new nationalism's clear need to mark Bishara and portray him as a pariah. The new nationalism needs Bishara as a pariah. His removal is part of the postfactum justification of the Jewish nationalist mobilization. It is also part of the effort to realign the political map after its huge drift to the right. If the Arab left can be portrayed as having gone beyond what the Jewish democratic system can tolerate as legitimate, then the right wing at the other extreme supposedly assumes a saner image. The whole cen-

---

* After his parliamentary immunity was lifted on November 7, 2001—the first time in its history the Knesset has lifted the immunity of a legislator for political speech—Bishara was indicted not only for illegally fostering the family reunions but, under the Prevention of Terror Ordinance, for two speeches: In June 2000 he congratulated Hizbollah for expelling the IDF from Lebanon, and in June 2001 in Syria, Bishara expressed general support for the intifada and urged a widening of the space for resistance between the two extremes of capitulation and all-out war.

tral bloc that had drifted to the right now represents the consensus. At its edges, beyond the fence, are a handful of Jews, Jewish terrorists and outlawed Kahanists on the one side, and a few leaders of the Arab population who incite their public to violence on the other. Only the blind will buy into this picture. Only the deaf will listen to this tune. But nationalism is blinding and deafening.

When occupation is both the *de facto* and the *de jure* state, the gap on the other side of the Green Line between *de facto* apartheid and *de jure* apartheid narrows. For gradually and almost without protest, the Israeli regime is shifting before our very eyes from *de facto* apartheid to *de jure* apartheid. The attempt to remove Bishara from the Israeli parliament is part of a maneuver intended to prepare and accelerate this shift and, in effect, to change the Israeli political system. The attempt to remove Bishara joins a proposed amendment to Basic Law: The Knesset designed to facilitate the disqualification of parties representing Israeli Palestinians and, moreover, to enable personal disqualification of candidates. The political implications of this law could do substantial damage to the parliamentary representation of Israel's Palestinian citizens. It also joins the series of legal investigations being conducted against Arab Members of the Knesset, and an even longer series of onslaughts portraying them as enemies and traitors and undermining the very legitimacy of their parliamentary activity.

On second thought, it seems that Azmi Bishara truly does constitute a threat to the new Israeli rule, the nationalistic rule that has perpetuated the temporariness of the occupation. The nationalists, including Attorney General Elyakim Rubinstein, argue their demand to remove Bishara's immunity and bring him to judgment in the parlance of "a democracy at risk." It is not the democracy of the Israeli state they are defending, of course, but the monopoly that Jewish citizens hold on defining the character of this state. They are defending their right to implement a rule of apartheid here. The defense of the threatened democracy is today represented by Azmi Bishara and most of the Arab Members of the Knesset, who depend upon the existence of a democratic regime in order to be able to defend themselves from the tyranny of the majority. Because he is such a prominent intellectual, original and daring, and free of the thought patterns that still cling to the Jewish–Palestinian conflict, Bishara is perhaps a spearhead in the defensive democratic camp. He exposes to Zionists the nationalistic limits of their liberalism. They regard Bishara's insistence on the Palestinian Israeli citizens' Arab nationality as dangerous. They cannot tolerate it. It requires them to admit that their nationalism is positioned high above their democratism, that it limits and systematically distorts their conception of democracy.

Azmi Bishara may be a spearhead in the defensive democratic camp. But the entire camp, it must be admitted, is today waging a rearguard war.

November 10, 2001

7

THE CHAMPION OF VIOLENT SOLUTIONS

Avi Shlaim

WHEN RUNNING FOR prime minister in February 2001, Ariel Sharon, Israel's ferocious hawk, tried to reinvent himself as a man of peace. Against the background of the intifada, which he himself had helped to trigger by his provocative visit to the Haram al-Sharif/Temple Mount, he ran on a ticket of "peace with security." In his first year in power, Sharon has achieved neither peace nor security but only a steady escalation of the violence. In the last two weeks Sharon has revealed once again his true colors as a man wedded to military force as the only instrument of policy.

The seventy-four-year-old Israeli leader has been involved at the sharp end of the confrontation with the Arabs for most of his life. The hallmarks of his career are mendacity, the most savage brutality toward Arab civilians, and a consistent preference for force over diplomacy to solve political problems. These features found their clearest expression in the invasion of Lebanon in 1982, which Sharon masterminded when he was defense minister in the Likud government headed by Menachem Begin.

The war that Sharon is currently waging on the West Bank, fraudulently named Operation Defensive Shield, is in some ways a replay of his war in Lebanon. It is directed against the Palestinian people; it stems from the same stereotype, that the Palestinians are terrorists; it is based on the same denial of Palestinian national rights; it employs the same strategy of savage and overwhelming military force; and it displays the same callous disregard for international public opinion, international law, the UN, and the norms of civilized behavior. Even the principal personalities are the same: Today, as in 1982, Ariel Sharon confronts his nemesis, Yasser Arafat. Sharon's hatred of the Palestinian leader runs so deep that recently he went as far as to express regret that he did not have Arafat shot during the siege of Beirut when an Israeli sniper had him in his gun sights.

The invasion of Lebanon was not a defensive war but a war of deception. Sharon obtained Cabinet approval for a limited military operation against the PLO forces in southern Lebanon. From the beginning, however, he planned a much bigger operation to serve broader geostrategic aims. The principal objective of Sharon's war was to destroy the PLO as a military and political organization, to break the backbone of Palestinian nationalism, to spread despair and despondency among the inhabitants of the West Bank, and to pave the way for its absorption into Greater Israel. A second objective was to give Israel's Maronite allies a leg up to power, and then compel them to sign a peace treaty with Israel. A third objective was to defeat and expel the Syrian army from Lebanon and to make Israel the dominant power in the Levant. Under Sharon's devious direction, an operation that was supposedly undertaken in self-defense developed into a merciless siege of Beirut and culminated in a horrendous massacre in the Palestinian refugee camps of Sabra and Shatila, which led to the removal of Sharon from his post at the Ministry of Defense.*

---

* After taking control of West Beirut in September 1982, the IDF, under direct orders from Defense Minister Sharon, surrounded the Sabra and Shatila refugee camps, whose armed fighters had been evacuated earlier under an agreement brokered by the United States. On September 16, the IDF brought into the camps its Lebanese Phalangist allies, who had carried out several massacres of Palestinian civilians during the civil war and who had repeatedly vowed to take revenge for the assassination days earlier of their leader, Bashir Gemayel. Illuminated by Israeli flares and observed by IDF soldiers atop nearby buildings, the Phalangists proceeded to slaughter between 1,000 and 3,000 Palestinian civilians. A subsequent Israeli commission of inquiry found Sharon both "indirectly" and "personally" responsible for the massacre.

In his crude but relentless propaganda war, Sharon tries to portray Arafat as the master terrorist who orchestrates the violence of the Palestinian security forces against Israel and secretly encourages suicide bombings by Hamas, Islamic Jihad, and the Al-Aqsa Martyrs Brigades. To be sure, Arafat is not above using violence to extract political concessions from the Israeli government. Nor has he done as much as he could to curb the activities of the Islamic militants. Yet Arafat is the leader who persuaded his movement to abandon the armed struggle and to adopt the political path in the struggle for independence. By signing the Oslo accord in 1993, and clinching it with a hesitant handshake, he and Yitzhak Rabin replaced mutual rejection with mutual recognition and undertook to resolve the outstanding differences between their two nations by peaceful means. Until the assassination of Rabin two years later, Arafat proved himself to be an effective partner on the road to peace. The subsequent decline and fall of the Oslo peace process was caused to a far greater degree by Israeli territorial expansionism than by Palestinian terrorism. Israeli settlements on the West Bank, which Sharon's national unity government continues to expand, are the root of the problem.

The other members of the Palestinian Authority are portrayed by Sharon as Arafat's confederates in crime, and, collectively, as a terrorist entity. Nothing could be further from the truth. The PA consists of a group of mainstream moderates who supported the historic compromise with Israel and who are deeply engaged in the process of state-building. It is an embryonic government, with an annual budget of $1 billion, charged with providing essential services to the 3,300,000 inhabitants of the territories. Its 150,000 employees include roughly 40,000 police and security officers. The rest are civil servants, school-teachers, welfare officers, doctors, hospital workers, and so on. Dismantling the PA would have catastrophic consequences for Palestinian society, and, ultimately, for the prospects of peace and security for Israel.

Ever the opportunist, Sharon was quick to jump on the bandwagon of America's war against terror in the aftermath of September 11. Under this banner, Sharon has embarked on a sinister attempt to destroy the infrastructure of a future Palestinian state. His real agenda is to put the clock back, to subvert what remains of the Oslo accords, to smash the Palestinians into the ground, and to extinguish once and for all their hope for independence and statehood. To add insult to injury, he wants to remove Yasser Arafat, the democratically elected leader and the symbol of the Palestinian revolution, and to replace him with a collaborationist regime that would meekly serve as a subcontractor charged with upholding Israeli security. What Sharon is unable or unwilling to comprehend is that security is not a zero-sum game and that it cannot be achieved by purely military means. The only hope of security for both communities lies in a return to the political track, something that this champion of violent solutions has always avoided like the plague. Consequently, Sharon's second war against the Palestinians, like his first, is doomed to failure from the start. If the history of this century-old conflict teaches us anything, it is that violence only breeds more violence.

Many people who do not necessarily support Sharon's brutal methods nevertheless have sympathy for Israel's predicament. They point out that the suicide bombings against innocent Israeli civilians predated the incursion of Israeli tanks into West Bank towns and villages. Israel's illegal occupation of the West Bank and Gaza, however, goes back to 1967 and constitutes the underlying cause of Palestinian frustration, hatred, and despair, of which the suicide bombers are only the cruelest manifestation. It is also pointed out that some segments of Palestinian society, notably the followers of Hamas and Islamic Jihad, deny altogether Israel's right to exist. These are, however, the extremist fringes, while the PA represents the Palestinian mainstream. The savage treatment meted out by Sharon to the Palestinian population is self-defeating precisely because it undermines the moderates and strengthens the extremists.

One of the most disturbing aspects of the current crisis is America's complicity in the Israeli onslaught against the Palestinian people and their institutions. One might have expected President George W. Bush to resume the evenhanded policy of his father's administration toward Arabs and Israelis. Instead, Bush Jr. has reverted to a blatantly pro-

Israeli policy reminiscent of the Reagan years. Although the United States is a signatory to the Oslo accord, President Bush has abandoned the Palestinian side to the tender mercies of Ariel Sharon. Sharon has held Arafat hostage in his headquarters in Ramallah, depriving him of food, water, medicines, and telephone lines. But, in what is almost a surreal story, the only concession that the American president has managed to extract from the truculent Israeli prime minister is a promise not to kill the Palestinian leader. The Israelis have destroyed much of Arafat's police force and security services, leaving him with a mobile phone. Under these conditions the embattled Palestinian leader does not have the means to prevent suicide attacks even if he had the will to do so.

In an apparent reversal of American policy a week ago, President Bush called on Sharon to pull out his troops from the Palestinian towns and villages. Sharon brushed aside the call, insisting they would stay for as long as is necessary to accomplish their mission of uprooting the infrastructure of terror. Secretary of State Colin Powell was dispatched to the region to broker a cease-fire and restore the political track. He is unlikely to get very far with Sharon unless he backs up his words with the threat to cut economic and military aid to Israel. The death toll in Operation Defensive Shield is over 200 Palestinians and 60 Israelis. How many more lives will have to be sacrificed before the Americans understand that General Sharon is part of the problem, not part of the solution?

April 13, 2002

Part Two

DISSENT

8

J'ACCUSE

Baruch Kimmerling

I ACCUSE MY prime minister, Ariel Sharon, of creating a process that will not only intensify the reciprocal bloodshed, but which may lead to a regional war and the partial or nearly complete ethnic cleansing of Arabs in "Greater Israel."

I accuse every Labor Party minister in the present Israeli government of partnership with the ultra-nationalist right wing in implementing its evil "vision."

I accuse the Palestinian leadership—and primarily Yasser Arafat—of shortsightedness so extreme that it has become a collaborator in Sharon's plans. If there is a second *nakba* (Palestinian catastrophe of 1948), this leadership, too, will carry partial responsibility.

I accuse the American government, and especially the administration of President George W. Bush, of complicity in the deaths of both Jews and Palestinians through its complete misunderstanding of the situation in the Middle East expressed by its willingness to give Sharon free rein in implementing a policy of "politicide" against the Palestinians. The United States government, as Israel's patron, bears full responsibility, not only for the recent escalation but for the coming bloodshed as well.

I accuse the military leadership of using its supposed expertise to incite public opinion against the Palestinians. Never before in Israel's history have so many high-ranking officers and members of military intelligence, some of whom cloak themselves as academics, taken part in public brainwashing. When a judicial committee of inquiry is established to investigate the 2002 catastrophe, they will have to be considered responsible along with the civilian leadership.

I accuse the Israeli electronic and print media of being submissive to various military spokespersons by granting them the access needed to exercise almost total control over an increasingly aggressive and bellicose public discourse. The military controls not only Palestinian cities, but Israeli radio and television as well.

I accuse those people, politicians and officers of all ranks, who order the black flag hoisted above them, and those who follow their unlawful orders. The late philosopher Yeshayahu Leibowitz was right: The occupation has ruined every good part of Israeli society and destroyed the moral and social infrastructures on which it rests. Let's stop this march of fools and build society anew, a society free of militarism, oppression, and the exploitation of other people.

I accuse everyone—mainly the majority of Jewish intellectuals in Israel and the United States—who sees and knows these things of doing nothing to prevent the impending catastrophe. The Sabra and Shatila massacres were nothing compared to what has happened—and what will happen—to us, Jews and Arabs, following this ethnic war.

And I accuse myself of knowing all this, yet crying little and keeping quiet too often.

February 1, 2002

9

TELL THE TRUTH, SHIMON

Gideon Levy

IN THE TWENTY-FOUR years of our acquaintance, four of which I spent working as your aide, this is the third time I have written you an open letter. In 1989, when you were finance minister in the Shamir government and the first intifada was raging, I used these pages to write "A Letter to a Former Boss." I told you then that "for the first time in your life, you have nothing left to lose—except the prospect of vanishing into thin air." This was after you kept silent in the face of the IDF's conduct in the intifada, in the face of the continuation of the occupation and Israel's stubborn refusal to recognize the PLO as the representative of the Palestinians. At the time, I believed that you thought differently from Yitzhak Shamir and Yitzhak Rabin (known then as the "bone-breaker"), but that you just weren't bold enough to speak up.*

Eleven years later, in 2000, I wrote you another open letter. This was after Oslo and the Rabin assassination, and after you again had lost an election—this time, to the office of president. I said then: "Many Israelis see you as a different person now. For them, you represent the hope of something else." And now, as I write to you again, I have to say: You no longer represent hope for anything.

The government of which you are a senior member, the foreign min-

---

* After the Palestinians rose up in the first intifada, Rabin—then defense minister—is said to have told soldiers to "break their bones."

ister, is no longer just a government of last resort in our history of governments of last resort; this government is a government of crime. And partnership in this crime is another matter. It is no longer possible to absolve you, to give you credit for Oslo, to understand that your heart aches over what is happening, and to know that you may even be bursting with rage over what is happening and refraining from speaking out, from shouting out, and most of all, from acting, only because of tactical considerations, which you understand better than anyone.

No, your silence and inaction can no longer be justified by any excuse: Shimon, you are a partner in crime. The fact that you might realize this in your heart and, from time to time, even utter some feeble words of condemnation, the fact that you are not prime minister and that America is giving carte blanche right now, the fact that most of the people think otherwise and that to quit and "chase after a *Ha'aretz* journalist," as you put it, would be pointless—all of these excuses make no difference. You continue to serve in a government with blood on its hands, whose outstretched hand is still busy killing and jailing and humiliating, and you are a partner in all of its deeds. Just as the Taliban foreign minister is a part of the Taliban regime, you are a part of the Sharon regime. Your responsibility does not fall far short of the prime minister's. It is equal to that of the defense minister and the chief of staff, whose actions you harshly criticize in private discussions. Always in private discussions only.

You say you heard about the assassination of Al-Aqsa Martyrs Brigades leader Raed Karmi, after three weeks of Palestinian quiet, on the radio. From your perspective, that's enough to exempt you from responsibility for the deed and even from having to express criticism of it. While the IDF was reoccupying Tulkarm [on January 21, 2002, the first seizure of an entire town since the outbreak of the intifada], you were with Bill Clinton. When asked about it, you mumbled something incoherent. Following the January house demolitions in Rafah, you bit your lip and kept silent. One could assume that the blowing up of the Voice of Palestine radio station [on January 19] was not your cup of tea either. But you bear the terrible responsibility for all of these things, for all of these actions that cannot be defined as anything other than war crimes.

Ask your brother-in-law, Professor Rafi Walden, the head of surgery at Sheba Medical Center, who sometimes travels to the territories as a volunteer with Physicians for Human Rights, and he'll tell you what you're a partner to. He'll tell you about the women in labor—not just one or two, not just the rare exception—who can't get to the hospital because of the cruelty of the IDF of which you were once so proud, and whose babies die right after they deliver them. He'll tell you about the cancer patients prevented from getting to Jordan for treatment. No, they cannot even go to Jordan—for "security reasons."

He'll tell you about the hospitals in Bethlehem that were shelled by the IDF. He'll tell you about the doctors and nurses who sleep in the hospital because they can't get home. He'll tell you about the dialysis patients forced to spend hours jostled about while traveling makeshift routes three times a week in a desperate attempt to reach the machines that their lives depend on. He'll tell you about the patients denied crucial medical treatment because of the closure and about the ambulances prevented from passing through checkpoints, even when they're carrying critically ill passengers. He'll tell you about the people who have died at the checkpoints and about those who died at home because they didn't dare to approach the checkpoints—which are now made up of menacing tanks in the middle of the road, or mounds of dirt and cement blocks that cannot be budged—even for someone on the brink of death.

You have imprisoned an entire people for over a year with a degree of cruelty unprecedented in the history of the Israeli occupation. Your government is trampling three million people, leaving them with no semblance of normal life. No going to the market, no going to work, no going to school, no visiting a sick uncle. Nothing. No going anywhere, and no coming back from anywhere. No day or night. Danger lurks everywhere, and everywhere there is another checkpoint, choking off life.

An entire nation already partly outstretched its hand in peace, no less than we have—you know this well. It has had its fill of suffering, from the *nakba* in 1948, through the 1967 occupation and the siege of 2002, and it wants exactly the same things that Israelis want for themselves—a little quiet, a little security, and a drop of national pride. To a man, this entire people now wakes up each morning to a gaping abyss of despair, unemployment, and deprivation—now with tanks parked at the end of the street, too.

You were always forgiven for all this—but no longer. Someone who is a partner in a government that deliberately sabotages every Palestinian effort to achieve quiet, that utterly humiliates their leaders, for whom vengeance is the sole motivating force, which cynically exploits the world's post–September 11 blindness and obtuseness to do as it pleases—can no longer be forgiven. True, you do not agree with everything this government wants to do, but what does that matter? You're inside—you're an accessory, as in any other crime. I sometimes see you answering a reporter's question about your government's latest despicable deed. The look on your face (and I'm pretty familiar with your expressions after all these years) suggests unease, even disgust. And then you give one of your evasive, hint-laden and not quite direct answers. You mumble something and try to extricate yourself by means of some awkward wordplay. Like what happened this week when you were standing next to Clinton and were asked about the occupation of Tulkarm and you said nothing—nothing—and just waited for the question to pass, to be left alone so you could go back to talking about peace and vision.

When asked about the assassinations, the demolitions, the humiliation of Arafat and his scandalous confinement, the destruction of the Dahaniya Airport or the festival of the munitions display in Eilat, you furrow your brow and give half an answer.* But that's not enough anymore.

Now is the time for a straight, honest and truthful answer—or nothing. Now is the time to say that the occupation of Tulkarm was a foolish move, that the assassination of Raed Karmi was intended to renew the

---

* On December 4, 2001, the IDF destroyed the Palestinian Authority's airport at Dahaniya, in Gaza. After seizing the *Karine A* on January 4, 2002, a ship laden with arms destined for the PA, Israel staged a public relations display of its contents at the Red Sea part of Eilat on January 6, with foreign ambassadors and diplomats trucked in to view the evidence.

violence and that the destruction of the houses in Rafah was a war crime—or to be Ariel Sharon. This is not the time for subtlety, for hidden meanings, for veiled criticism in private—because, here on the outside, a terrible disaster is under way, and a great ill wind is blowing and laying waste to everything.

Shall I give you an example? A few days ago, you were quoted as saying (privately, again) that it was hard for you to criticize the government's actions when the United States wasn't doing so. What kind of pathetic excuse is that? What does the fact that there is a predatory administration in the United States that has no counterbalancing power in the world, that does as it pleases and lets Israel do as it pleases, have to do with your principled positions? What does that have to do with the good of Israel? What does that have to do with basic values of justice and morality?

Perhaps you might take just one day of vacation, which you so rarely do, and visit the occupied territories. Have you ever actually seen the Qalandiyah checkpoint [between Jerusalem and Ramallah], even once? Have you seen what happens there? Do you think that you can do your job without seeing the Qalandiyah checkpoint? Do you understand that you are responsible for what goes on there? Do you understand that any foreign minister of a state that puts up these checkpoints bears responsibility for their existence?

Then you could go to the village of Yamoun and meet Heira Abu Hassan and Amiya Zakin, who lost their babies three weeks ago when IDF soldiers wouldn't let their cars through the checkpoint, while they were in labor and bleeding. Listen to their terrible stories. And what will you tell them? That you're sorry? That it shouldn't have happened? That it's part of the war on terror? That it's shocking? That maybe it's Shaul Mofaz's fault and not yours? The IDF spokesman hasn't even expressed regret about these two instances, not to mention any criminal investigation. He only confirmed that one occurred and said he "didn't know" about the other.

And equally important, what will you say about our soldiers who behave this way? That it's because of national security? That the Palestinians are to blame? Or Arafat? The truth, Shimon, is that you bear responsibility for the deaths of those two babies. Because you were silent. Because you sat in this government.

These are terrible times. But worse is yet to come. The cycle of violence and hatred has far from reached its peak. All the injustices and evil perpetrated against the Palestinians will eventually blow up in our faces. A people that is abused this way for years will explode one day in a terrible fury, even worse than what we see now. And meanwhile we have the soldiers going into the radio station, laying explosives and blowing the place to kingdom come—without stopping to ask why.

These soldiers are the bearers of bad tidings, not only for their victims, but for their dispatchers as well. Soldiers who destroy dozens of homes belonging to refugees, with all their meager possessions inside, without a moment's hesitation—and certainly no refusal to carry out such blatantly illegal orders—are not good soldiers, even for their country. Pilots who bomb targets in the heart of populated cities, tank operators who point their guns at women trying to get to the hospital to give birth in the middle of the night, and Border Police officers who abuse women and youngsters are not a good portent of things to come. They all attest to the loosening of restraint that derives from a total loss of direction.

Yes, this year we have lost our way. You have joined forces with a prime minister who is Israel's most veteran warmonger, and no one can say for sure what your intentions are. And with a brainwashed public that speaks with frightening uniformity, you have it easy. Ever since another member of your party, Ehud Barak, intentionally shattered the peace camp, you've been able to do practically as you pleased. The IDF no longer investigates any war crime, and the legal system approves every injustice that comes wrapped in the mantle of security. The whole world is busy struggling against terror, the press hides its face, and the public doesn't want to hear, doesn't want to see, and doesn't want to know. It only wants revenge. And under cover of this darkness and with the backing of a person of your stature, the occupation has become a machine of crime and evil.

Naturally, you'll say: What can I do? I wasn't elected prime minister. And I wasn't elected chairman of the Labor Party. I'm not even the defense minister. You're right: In this government you cannot do anything and you are not doing anything. Which is exactly why you never should have become a member of it. You'll say: I have influence; I rein things in, I'm a moderating force, I'm trying. Nonsense. It couldn't be much worse than it is now, so where exactly have you exerted your influence and what are you preventing from happening? Did you ever imagine that you would be sitting in a government that would reoccupy parts of Area A completely unhindered?

Just think what would have happened had you got up and loudly resigned from this government and told the world what is (perhaps) in your heart. The Nobel Prize laureate versus the crimes of the Sharon government. Imagine if you had gone to Ramallah, to Yasser Arafat, who is under siege there, and taken to the street together, faced the Israeli tanks and called for their removal and for a cease-fire. True, the sky wouldn't have fallen—the occupation wouldn't have ended and the closure of Jenin would not have been lifted, but real cracks would have been opened in the moral, political and international basis of this currently immune government. Imagine if you had said: Yes, the house demolitions are a war crime. Yes, a state that has lists of assassination targets is not a state of law. Yes, installing a checkpoint that causes people to die is an act of terror. No, the Palestinians are not the only ones to blame for this orgy of blood. Yes, we have a chief of staff who is a danger to democracy. Yes, we have a defense minister and Labor Party chairman who is the government's contractor for assassinations and house demolitions. Yes, we have a prime minister who only wants to occupy, to avenge, to kill, to expel, to demolish, and to uproot, and he has no other plan in mind.

That's what you think, isn't it? If it is, then say so, for God's sake. And if not, then your place really is with this government and we who once believed in you made a dreadful mistake. And please don't say that you're being made a punching bag once again. You're not. Ever since Oslo, you were the embodiment of our hopes. And these have been disappointed.

Time is short, Shimon. Not just for you, but for all of us. We are standing on the verge of the abyss. If you wait until Benjamin Ben-

Eliezer, Ephraim Sneh, Ra'anan Cohen, Dalia Itzik [the other Labor ministers in Sharon's cabinet] and their like come up with another sneaky resigning-from-the-government-for-election-purposes deal, you might just find yourself kicked into oblivion by them. You know that they've been itching to be rid of you for some time now. And even if you do make a stand now, it may just be too late. Everyone may already be too disappointed in you and there may be no way to rebuild the ruin brought about by Sharon.

But the only way for you to add one more meaningful accomplishment to your rich biography is not just to get up now and resign from this government, which you may be compelled to do at some point anyway, but to do it while speaking out loud and clear, and telling Israelis all that you think about everything that is happening, especially about the evil we are perpetrating with our own hands. Once more in your life, try to build something new—not an atomic reactor or an aircraft industry, of which we already have more than enough. Now, against all the odds, try to build a radical Israeli peace camp, to make something out of nothing. Is it too far-fetched to believe that you still see things differently than the rest of your colleagues in the government? Tell the truth, Shimon.

January 25, 2002

10

YOU CAN CONTINUE WITH THE LIQUIDATIONS

Shulamit Aloni

IN VIEW OF the developments of the past two days, it is hard to find in the government's actions justification, or even a hint of intelligence.

After the destruction of the houses in Rafah and Jerusalem the Palestinians continued to act with restraint. Sharon and his army minister, who apparently feared that they would have to return to the negotiating table, decided to do something, so they liquidated Raed Karmi. They knew that there would be a response, and that we would pay the price in the blood of citizens. Thus it turned out that the blood of the celebrants in Hadera is apparently a reasonable price to pay to maintain the ferment in the occupied territories.*

There are no negotiations, there will not be peace, the settlements will expand and get stronger, and we will be able to continue liquidating, demolishing, and uprooting.

---

* On January 10, 2002, the Israeli army bulldozed fifty-four homes in Gaza's Rafah refugee camp, leaving more than 500 homeless, in reaction to the killing of four Israeli soldiers by Hamas guerrillas at an IDF outpost in Gaza the day before. Four days later, the Israelis destroyed nine Palestinian homes in East Jerusalem. On January 14, Israel assassinated Raed Karmi, a leader of the Al-Aqsa Martyrs Brigades, in Tulkarm. In retaliation, a Tulkarm gunman from the Al-Aqsa Martyrs Brigades attacked a bat-mitzvah celebration in Hadera, killing six and wounding thirty, the first such suicide attack inside Israel in more than a month.

HEART AND KIDNEY SPECIALISTS

Over the course of the year 2000 the Palestinian Authority invested over two billion shekels in development, construction, and tourism. Those investments were made with representatives of the donor states and under their supervision; we can assume that whoever is investing in this way is not preparing an intifada. Whoever has seen the construction and development in the territories of the Authority, and who sees destruction and ruin today, and proceeds to say that all this is due to Arafat's murderous and destructive nature, is an incorrigible demagogue.

Since Arik Sharon was elected Prime Minister, with Fuad [Benjamin Ben-Eliezer] as Defense Minister, and Shaul Mofaz as Chief of Staff, we hear everywhere what Arafat is thinking, what he is planning, that he is an irrelevant liar, that he has fulfilled his role but is doing everything to destroy us in stages. Before those potentates carry out their plot and eliminate the strongest and most awesome army in the Middle East, it is our duty to bomb, destroy, liquidate, crush, uproot, expel, plug wells, and to harass at checkpoints—for the sake of the "peace with security" that Sharon and his ministers want to bring us.

But since the chief of staff and his generals are not psychologists and not heart and kidney specialists, and since the shamefulness of their actions tears the heart, I decided to go to Arafat personally and hear his version; and maybe to tell him not all of us are Sharon.

Arafat repeated his words that we Israelis are trying to forget: That already in 1988 the institutions of the PLO accepted UN Resolutions 242 and 338—that is, the Green Line borders—and from their point of view that means that they gave up on greater Palestine and recognized the existence of the State of Israel. He repeated that if Rabin had not been murdered, there would already be peace between the two peoples. One may disbelieve, but it is hard to deny that the man was murdered by "opponents of peace" among us.

Arafat also spoke of the economic hardship, of the hunger and poverty that we are imposing on his people. He recounted that when Rabin decided on closure, he passed $15 million to the Authority to pay salaries. Whereas now, for the past eighteen months Israel has held 900 million shekels belonging to the Palestinians, in addition to the fact that many communities have been converted to internment camps, which are also starvation camps.

THE "ALL-POWERFUL" AND THE "KING OF ISRAEL"

Israelis say that Arafat can control Hamas and Islamic Jihad and subdue them. In view of the many years I have been living, I can recall that David Ben-Gurion, who stood at the head of the leaders of the organized Yishuv [the Zionist Jewish community in British Mandate Palestine], could not restrain the Lehi [the "Stern gang," of which Yitzhak Shamir was a member] or Etzel [the Irgun, led by Menachem Begin] "terrorist" organizations—which continued with the killing, the bombing and the liquidations against the British and Arabs. Sharon apparently will not rest and will not be silent until the "all-powerful" Arafat launches a civil war among his people, who are under the boots of Israeli soldiers at checkpoints and under the settlers who rob their land.

Whoever claims that the settlements are Israel's catastrophe from a security and economic point of view is not an anti-Semite but a patriot. Whoever says that this government is committing crimes against humanity is not an anti-Semite but an honest and humane person. Whoever condemns the demolition of houses in Rafah and Jerusalem, opposes the provocative liquidations and fostering of ferment in the area so that we can avoid going to the negotiating table, does so out of love for their homeland.

What goes around comes around. The intifada will continue and Sharon, the "king of Israel," along with Avigdor Lieberman, Benny Elon, Uzi Landau, Tzahi Hanegbi [at the time, the right wing of Sharon's cabinet] and others will continue to wave the flag of righteousness and the flag of Greater Israel.

I went to Arafat in order to tell him that in spite of everything there are still many in Israel who will not let despair destroy the hope of peace. It is incumbent on all who believe in the cause of a just peace to work together to conquer injustice, greed and power-worship to bring peace and prosperity to the two peoples.

January 18, 2002

11

A JOURNEY TO BEIT JALA

Yigal Bronner

THE SKY IS overcast, and it begins to drizzle on the hills surrounding Bethlehem as we arrive at the mound blocking the entrance to the village of Beit Jala. We drive slowly—a convoy of about a hundred cars and four trucks, all loaded with food and medicine—and then come to a halt. The people of Beit Jala have been under curfew for the last month, with no end in sight. Now, for the first time in several days, the curfew has been lifted for a few hours, allowing them to stock up supplies (not that the shops in the village have much to offer). Several dozen residents decide to spend this precious time on coming to the roadblock in order to welcome us.

We shake hands and embrace, and then get down to work. The food in the cars is unloaded and passed over the mound to a truck waiting on the other side. Several boxes full of medicine—urgently needed in a hospital for the mentally ill—pass hands as well. Three of the trucks continue to other destinations (along a nearby road, controlled by the army), to villages and refugee camps in the Bethlehem area whose situation is even worse than Beit Jala's.

Meanwhile, as in similar convoys organized by Ta'ayush, an Arab-Jewish group that combines humanitarian aid with political action, a gathering is organized. The mayor of Beit Jala is the first speaker. I listen to his description of life under curfew and constant siege as I pass through the crowd. I am looking for the parents of Laith, a nine-year-old from Beit Jala. A few months ago, during a previous round of violence, Laith was smuggled out of his enclosed village by friends, and enjoyed a picnic and a visit to a theme park in Israel. For one day he was like any other kid, free to run outside and play. This is how I got to know and like him; my family had joined him on his one day of freedom, and my six-year-old son, Amos, was one of his playmates.

Now I get to meet his parents, a charming couple. It is an emotional moment. For a brief while we have what resembles a normal conversation among parents. They inquire about Amos, I about Laith. But Laith's childhood is by no means normal. He has been confined to his home for four weeks now, without a single breath of fresh air. Even now, his parents don't allow him out. Too risky. They left him with his aunt, and must soon return for another unknown period of house arrest. We part with the hope of meeting soon, perhaps under better circumstances. I try to imagine my son, Amos, in Laith's situation, and find it hard to do. What do you tell a boy his age? How does one explain the need to stay at home? To be patient? What does he think when he sees soldiers roaming the village streets, imposing curfew and taking away his freedom?

Speaking of soldiers, they surround us from all sides. Yuri, one of the convoy's organizers, is now speaking and addressing the military. He tells the soldiers that they are unwelcome here. He urges them to leave and return one day as guests rather than occupiers and colonizers, and wishes them a safe trip home. He tells them about the misery they are inflicting on the Palestinian civilians. About the hunger and poverty. About the feeling of the farmer who helplessly sees his crops rotting, unable to tend to them. Yuri is followed by Liora. She speaks of the Palestinian women—whose husbands have been detained by the army, and who are now single mothers caring for their children—as the true victims and heroines of this war.

The soldiers stand around us, revealing no emotion. I don't know what they are thinking. But it is clear they wish to be seen as part of our event. By allowing humanitarian aid to pass, they hope to prove that they are "the most humanitarian army in the world." One of them is even documenting the event with a videocamera, presumably for PR purposes. Just a fortnight ago, the army spokesperson used footage of a similar food convoy headed for the devastated Jenin camp as proof of the humane nature of the Israeli troops (who were meanwhile bulldozing homes on their inhabitants). What the spokesman neglected to mention was that the army stopped the thirty-plus trucks en route to Jenin, despite its promise to let them through, and allowed only a trickle of supplies to pass.

With this recent bitter experience in mind, we are determined not to leave Beit Jala until we are certain that the trucks have passed all of the military checkpoints. When news arrives from the drivers that they have reached their destination, we begin to wrap things up. We part from our hosts who must hurry home before the curfew is reimposed, and send the long convoy of cars back to Israel. A few of us remain to wait for the returning truck drivers. As it turns out, though, our day's adventures are not quite over.

On the way back from Bethlehem, the Israeli military stops one of the empty trucks. Four armored vehicles surround it, a tank points its cannon at it, and the soldiers aim guns at the driver and force him out. We call the driver on the mobile phone; he sounds afraid. The soldiers who gave the truck its entry-permit at the checkpoint promise to release it, but there seems to be a communication problem between them and the troops in Bethlehem.

The minutes go by. It is now late afternoon, and the sun is about to set. The truck has not yet been released, and we stand waiting, talking with the driver every few minutes to calm him down. It is cold. But, as we try to warm ourselves, we get another chilling glimpse of the occupation. A small army pickup arrives at the checkpoint with three Palestinians lying in the back. They are in their fifties; their arms and legs are tightly tied, and their eyes are covered. It is quite obvious that they are not at the top of the army's most-wanted list, for they are left unattended. The army base is just around the corner, but no one seems in a hurry to take them in and interrogate them. They simply lie like cattle.

We approach the soldiers and ask them at least to uncover the detainees' eyes. They refuse. An argument ensues, in which the soldiers insist that their mode of action is the most humane. Nonetheless, they prohibit us from photographing the men. After some discussion, they allow us to give them water and cigarettes. We catch a brief word with them. They are from the Deheisheh refugee camp. They have no idea where they are now. I don't know why they were arrested. But being a Palestinian man these days automatically makes you suspect, and the most trivial actions, such as leaving your home, turn you into a criminal.

At last, the truck arrives and we embrace the driver, the true hero of the day. We learn that while passing through Bethlehem a large group of residents desperately jumped on top of one truck, grabbing whatever they could. "They were not thieves," the driver, a Palestinian citizen of Israel, explains, "they were simply hungry. One old lady ran after us for a kilometer just to get one pack of rice. I saw very difficult sights," he added. "It is an altogether different world there, on the other side of the army checkpoint." We exchange a few more stories, take a photo next to the empty truck, and leave for Jerusalem. As we leave, the three men are still lying in the military pickup truck, tied and blindfolded.

Four cars and one truck drive quickly on the empty road. As the beautiful hills of Bethlehem turn to dusk, we hit the last army checkpoint. The soldiers manning it insist on stopping the Palestinians among us. They are, after all, Arabs. They take their Israeli IDs away for "inspection," which seems to go on forever. They tell us that they have called the police to make sure their "record is clean." We wait together. Another hour passes. It is dark and the wind is freezing. Finally, we decide to protest. Two of us park our cars so as to block traffic to and from the nearby settlement, insisting that if we are not allowed to travel, neither will they. This stirs some commotion. The officer in charge arrives, IDs are returned, and we are free to go. We learn that the police had approved our entry a while ago but the soldiers wanted to keep us waiting longer, for the fun of it.

I arrive home a bit after seven. Galila is putting the kids to bed. I kiss Amos and tell him I met Laith's parents, and that they say Hi. I tell him some but not all of what I experienced. I put him and my toddler-daughter, Naomi, to sleep. Then I pause to think. I know I saw only the surface, had only a tiny glimpse of what is really going on in occupied

Palestine. I haven't seen the really devastating scenes of Jenin and Nablus. But what I saw, heard, and experienced—the child confined to his home for a month, the old lady running after the food truck, the men lying on the floor of the army vehicle, the soldiers humiliating my Palestinian friends at the roadblock—all that was quite educational. It allowed me to understand that what Israel has been destroying in Palestine is much more than the infrastructure of terrorism. It has been destroying the agricultural, educational, medical, and road infrastructure; it has been eroding goodwill and undermining whatever is left of the Palestinian desire for peace. It has been sowing hunger, poverty, humiliation, and hatred, all of which only serve to fortify the infrastructure of terrorism. I go to sleep thinking of Amos and Laith, hoping that they can somehow grow up as friends.

April 26, 2002

12

AN ISRAELI IN PALESTINE

Jeff Halper

AT 7:30 THIS morning, as I was about to travel with other members of the Israeli Committee Against House Demolitions to the besieged town of Beit Umar, near Hebron, where tons of produce cannot be transported to market and are rotting while the inhabitants face severe hunger, I got a call that six bulldozers accompanied by hundreds of soldiers were entering the Shuafat refugee camp to the north of Jerusalem. The ICAHD members proceeded to Beit Umar, while Arik Ascherman of Rabbis for Human Rights, Liat Taub, a student and ICAHD staff member, Gadi Wolf, a conscientious objector who just served time in jail, and I headed for Shuafat.

On the way I had that sinking feeling of powerlessness mixed with outrage that always accompanies me to events like this—an equal mixture of responsibility, anger at the injustice, the fundamental unfairness of it all, and helplessness in the face of an unmoving, uncaring, cruel, and supremely self-righteous system of oppression. On the way we all worked our cell phones, Arik calling the press, me calling the embassies and consulates (both the American and European consulates are very responsive and forthcoming), Liat and Gadi calling our lists of activists to join us, keeping in touch with our Palestinian partners as well. Meir Margalit, a Jerusalem City Council member from the Meretz party who has been a steadfast ally, and Salim Shawamreh, our Palestinian partner who lived in Shuafat before building a home of his own in nearby Anata, which was demolished three times, waited for us.

We passed through the familiar and profoundly banal streets of West Jerusalem, with people all around going about their "normal" lives, passing the thousands of apartments built for Israelis in East Jerusalem (50,000 more or less, so that the 200,000 Israelis living in East Jerusalem today outnumber the Palestinian population), neat stone-faced apartment blocks framed with trees, shrubbery, and lawns, served by wide streets and sidewalks. Once past the neighborhood/ settlement of French Hill, however, the landscape changes, though we remain within the city of Jerusalem as defined by Israel in 1967. The hillsides become barren, strewn with shells of old cars and garbage. The houses are small, scattered, and made of unattractive cement blocks. No trees, no lawns, no sidewalks, certainly no parks—just narrow, dusty, potholed streets with no streetlights. People, kids walking on the shoulders, competing for space with minivans and old cars. The Third World just a hundred meters down the road, and in the same city.

And then the soldiers. As we approached the main entrance to the camp, we saw hundreds of soldiers, Border Police and regular police (Uzi Landau, our minister of "Internal Security" and one of the Likud's Rejectionist Front on peace, said Sunday in the *Ma'ariv* newspaper that he will provide all the police the Jerusalem municipality needs to demolish houses). Some were mounted on horseback, others drove about in the dozens of military jeeps that blocked all the entrances to the camp and patrolled its maze of alleyways, their guns hanging from the doors and windows. We parked and walked in, careful to stay in touch with Salim, who sent some people to escort us, uncertain how Israelis would be received at such a time. We were received well. Walking with our hosts I was struck by how "normal" life was continuing. Kids played in the street, men worked in the garages along the roads, women went about their business. Just a few minutes away houses were being demolished and the camp was completely overrun by soldiers, yet people had developed a way to continue their lives no matter what. *Sumud,* steadfast, is the Arabic name for it.

We walked through the crowded camp of some 25,000 people, finally coming out on the top of a hill overlooking the periphery of the
camp and, across the wadi, the narrow valley, the Jerusalem settlement
of Pisgat Ze'ev looming over Shuafat from the opposite hill. Juxtaposed
in this way, the injustice virtually hits you in the face. Here was a
crowded camp, layers of jerry-built concrete homes separated by the
narrowest of alleyways, leading down a slope where the raw sewage of
the camp flowed to the houses where the bulldozers had already started
their demolition work (you could hear the hack-hack-hack of the
pneumatic drills collapsing the concrete roofs), and then, just a couple
hundred meters away, the massive modern housing project of Pisgat
Ze'ev ("Ze'ev's Summit," named after the Likud's founding father, Ze'ev
Jabotinsky) with its manicured lawns and trees. And, separating these
two worlds, the stream of sewage down below (Pisgat Ze'ev has its own
closed sewage system, thank you), and the "security road" where the
army patrols at night, guarding the residents of Pisgat Ze'ev from their
neighbors.

In order to avoid the soldiers and police, we walked through the alleyways and down the slope, sloshing through the sewage to come up to
the scene of the demolitions. The army and police had their backs
turned to us as they guarded the bulldozers and drills from the angry
Palestinian crowd, including the frantic home owners who were about
to see their life savings go up in dust. We quickly ran to the bulldozers
and lay down in front of them. A symbolic action, to be sure, but one
that created a scene and gave news photographers something to
"shoot." (Because we are Israelis, we have the privilege of being shot
only by cameras.) For the soldiers our actions are simply stupid and
incomprehensible, and they cart us away unceremoniously. We don't
bother to argue with them or explain to them; it is enough that we act as
vehicles for getting the images of demolitions out to the world. Later,
when the reporters talk to us, we can explain what is happening and
why it is unjust and oppressive. Our comments will find their way into
official reports; this evening the U.S. State Department officially de-
plored the demolitions, and we know that European and other governments take note. That is our role. Helplessness in the face of

overwhelming force and callousness, yet faith that all of you, once you know, will generate the international pressures necessary to end the occupation, once and for all. As an Israeli, and speaking strictly for myself, I have despaired of ever convincing my own people that a just peace is the way. Israelis may passively accept dictates from outside, but a just peace will not come from within Israeli society.

Arik, Liat and Gadi are hauled away in a police jeep, presumably arrested. There isn't room for me, so I'm left sitting in the dust, my clothes torn, just a little bruised from the manhandling and being hauled over the rocks, but glad to have an opportunity to take pictures of the demolitions and to relay the ongoing developments to reporters. The Palestinians across the way either watch impassively, helplessly, or, when the bulldozers leave the last rubble heap and approach their homes, react by climbing to the roof, yelling at the soldiers (women even dare push them sometimes), occasionally throwing stones. At these times the soldiers' reactions are quick and violent: High-powered rifles are aimed at the protesters, people are shoved into police vans, tear gas is thrown (sometimes inside the houses, though the instructions on the canisters, produced by Federal Laboratories in Pennsylvania, clearly state "for outdoor use only"). People often get shot, though that didn't happen today. The soldiers and police, who just a few minutes before were joking with each other (from conversations with them over the years, I haven't encountered any who see anything wrong with what is happening, or have any problem blaming the Palestinians for the demolitions of their own houses, and who refer to what they are doing as "work"), suddenly become violently enraged. As if the Palestinians have the chutzpah to resist, as if they are the criminals, as if "we" now have an opportunity to get even with "them," to extract revenge for not accepting our occupation. And one by one the houses are systematically torn down, this one a shell not yet completed, that one a four-story building intended to provide decent shelter (at last) to thirty members of an extended family (I watch the grandfather crying on the side, wiping his tears with his kaffiya, trying not to lose his dignity altogether). Fourteen "structures" (as Israel calls them). By 12:30 the operation is over. The soldiers are in no hurry to leave; indeed, at least a hundred more arrive in the camp as the demolitions are winding down. Israel loves to leave the Palestinians "messages."

In the end an army jeep came and I was tossed in the back. We drove up the security road to Pisgat Ze'ev, where I was told to go home. Walking over to a bus stop, dirty, smelly from the sewage, my clothes torn, a woman asks me what happened. Reluctantly I tell her that I was trying to resist the demolition of some of the homes of her neighbors in Shuafat, nodding in the direction of the camp. The reaction was painfully predictable. "Terrorists! They're trying to move their houses into our neighborhood! Why don't they build with permits, like we do? They don't pay taxes and expect free houses and services! This is our country. When I came here from Morocco . . ." The bus pulls up, we get on and she tells the driver: "Leave him off in Shuafat. They'll kill him there." (Though Mayor Ehud Olmert declares at every opportunity that Jerusalem is a "united" city, there are no municipal buses to Shuafat or most of East Jerusalem—or streetlights, or sewers, or postal service, or even street names. An invisible city to Israelis.)

Fourteen houses demolished out of twenty-five that received demolition orders yesterday (the owners were given no chance to appeal to the courts). Some 2,000 demolition orders outstanding in East Jerusalem alone, another 2,000 in the West Bank and Gaza. Eight thousand Palestinian houses demolished since 1967, 500 during the course of the second intifada, since September. And *we* will not resume negotiations until *they* stop the "violence."

I wind my way back to Shuafat. Arik, Liat and Gadi made it back before me and managed to get arrested formally this time (they were released an hour or so later). I meet up with Salim and Meir and we plan an "action" for the next day or so, perhaps the rebuilding of one of the houses, if the Shuafat people are willing. As I head home for a shower and a change of clothes, I hear Olmert on the radio: "You cannot build in any city in the world without a permit. They want to build on green open space that we set aside for their own benefit. The Palestinians tell me quietly that they support my efforts to fight illegal building. I don't demolish homes in West Jerusalem because Jews only build illegal porches, not entire houses." Et cetera. All lies. But being one of the few

Israelis that ever experiences Palestine, I find it impossible to convey to my own people, my own neighbors (good people all, even the Likud and Shas* voters), what occupation means, why they should feel responsible and resist with me. Israel is a self-contained bubble with a self-contained and exclusively Jewish narrative. The struggle continues.

July 2001

---

* The right-wing Shas party represents the Sephardic Orthodox community in the Knesset.

13

THE ENEMY WITHIN

Neve Gordon

"FOR ISRAEL, SEPTEMBER 11 was a Hanukkah miracle," *Ha'aretz*'s political analyst recently quoted Israeli officials as having said. Thousands of American fatalities are considered—in this cynical world—a godsend because their deaths helped shift international pressure from Israel onto the Palestinians, while allowing the Israeli government to pursue its regional objectives unobstructed. Indeed, ever since September 11 the United States has supported Israel's actions. The Sharon-led government has exploited this change of mood in the Bush administration and is determined to wreak havoc on the Palestinian Authority, precluding the possibility that an independent Palestinian state will emerge anytime soon. Recent events suggest that Sharon is interested in unseating Arafat, with the hope of precipitating an intra-Palestinian conflict, perhaps even a civil war. Israel, so the twisted logic goes, can then help set up a puppet government while changing the West Bank's territorial demarcation—the Lebanon debacle revisited.

As the cycle of violence consumes more lives, many an Israeli has lost the ability to think clearly. According to a poll that appeared in the country's largest newspaper, *Yediot Ahronot*, 74 percent of Israelis are in favor of the government's assassination policy. But when asked if they thought the assassinations were effective, 45 percent claimed that they actually increase Palestinian terrorism, 31 percent stated that they have no effect on terrorism, and only 22 percent averred that assassinations help deter terrorism. Almost half of all Israelis believe that the government's reaction to terrorism is inimical to their own interests, but continue, nonetheless, to support assassinations.

This suggests that a visceral instinct has taken over the national psyche, marginalizing and repressing all forms of political reasoning. In the *Republic*, Plato warns against the ascendancy of feelings and emotions in the public sphere, claiming that these traits characterize the emergence of despotic rule. Many years from now people may ask (just as we wonder about other times and places) how it was that a whole population did not realize what was happening.

To be sure, what is left of the Israeli peace camp has been trying to mount some kind of viable opposition. Weekly protests in front of the Prime Minister's house and hundreds of Jews and Arab citizens of Israel breaking the military siege by transferring basic foodstuffs to Palestinian villages are just two of the manifestations of political resistance. These activities, however, have not managed to displace the spirit of war.

There are many reasons why the Israeli peaceniks have had little, if any, impact on local politics. While most commentators mention the dramatic decrease in the peace camp's numbers following its disappointment with Arafat, no one has discussed the effect Israel's fascistization has had on the political scene. Indeed, Israel's gravest danger today is not the Palestinian Authority or even Hamas and Islamic Jihad, but the one it faces from within: fascism.

The fascistization of politics takes many forms, some more apparent than others. Perhaps most conspicuous is the dramatic change in the Israeli landscape. A few months following the eruption of the second intifada, thousands of billboards, posters, bumper stickers and graffiti began to appear, with slogans like "No Arabs, No Assaults," "Expel Arafat," "Kahane Was Right," and "The Criminals of Oslo Should Be Brought to Justice." * It was shocking, at the time, that slain Prime Minister Yitzhak Rabin had been criminalized by his own people.

* Rabbi Meir Kahane, an American who founded the Jewish Defense League in the 1960s and later immigrated to Israel, founded the Kach party, which advocated expulsion of the Palestinians. He was assassinated in New York in 1990.

But, as it turned out, this was just the beginning. Stickers stating "No Leftists, No Assaults" were printed to accompany the ones exclaiming "No Arabs, No Assaults," while little by little a whole new brand of posters directed against Palestinian citizens of Israel appeared on the scene: "Do Not Employ Arabs," "Enemies Should Not Be Offered a Livelihood," "We Will Assist Those Who Do Not Provide Work for Arabs." One poster even provided a detailed list of taxi companies that employ Arab citizens and companies that don't; Jewish history, so it seems, has been forgotten.

This kind of blatant racism is now common in Israel; it feeds off the widespread fear of suicide bombings, which have also managed to change the Jerusalem landscape. Downtown streets are almost empty, and most businesses have been seriously hurt because of the dramatic decline in clientele. One poll suggests that 67 percent of Israelis have reduced the number of times they leave their home. The only companies that have been thriving in recent months are security firms. Every supermarket, bank, theater, and café now employs private guards whose duty is to search customers as they enter the building.

One of the effects of this new practice is that profiling has become ubiquitous. Arab-looking residents refrain from using public transportation and from going to Jewish neighborhoods and shopping centers. It is not unusual when driving in the city to see groups of Arab men being searched at gunpoint by Israeli police, their faces against the wall and their hands in the air. Meanwhile, the Israeli secret service routinely intercepts the e-mails of peace groups and often obstructs solidarity meetings or protests in the West Bank by declaring whole regions "closed military zones." Peace activists are "invited" to meetings with the secret service, where they are "warned" about their activities. For over a year, the Gaza Strip has been totally closed off to Israelis from the peace camp—including Knesset Members; only Jewish settlers, journalists, and soldiers can now enter the region. Over one million Palestinians residing in the Strip have been locked up for a year and a half now in what constitutes the world's biggest jail, and no Israeli can visit them.

Torture, which was finally banned in September 1999 after a decade-long struggle in the Supreme Court, has reemerged with a vengeance. According to the Israeli Public Committee Against Torture, the secret service has not only replaced outlawed methods of torture with new ones, but ill-treatment, police brutality, poor prison conditions and the prohibition of legal counsel are now widespread. B'Tselem, the Israeli Information Center for Human Rights in the Occupied Territories, has documented the torture of Palestinian minors, while the Association for Civil Rights and other organizations have appealed to the Supreme Court against the new practice of holding suspects incommunicado. In the past year, however, the Supreme Court has rejected all human rights appeals that in any way relate to the lives of the Palestinian population in the occupied territories.

Ever since September 2000, much of the Israeli media, which had been well known for its critical edge, has turned into a government organ. For Israeli television viewers, Palestinian suffering is virtually nonexistent, while attacks on Jews are graphically portrayed, replayed time and again, thus rendering victimhood the existential condition of the Israeli Jew. The deeply rooted victim syndrome has been manipulated over the past year in order to rally the public around the flag.

Along the same lines, almost no criticisms of the government's policies make their way into the mainstream media. On the one hand, Jewish opposition leaders and peace groups find it extremely difficult to get their opinions aired. On the other hand, the media is actively assisting the state not only in legitimizing its actions, but also in delegitimizing Israel's Palestinian citizens.

The exclusion of almost a fifth of Israel's citizenry from the *demos* is accomplished by attacking their leaders. Jewish cabinet ministers and other Knesset Members repeatedly refer to the Arab representatives as Arafat's agents, collaborators, and a fifth column. Joining the fanfare, newspapers, television, and radio have marked them not only as "other" but also as enemies, which serves to justify the harassment they are currently undergoing.

In the past year, six out of ten Arab Knesset Members from opposition parties have undergone police investigation for "anti-Israeli" statements they made during political speeches, while the immunity of one has already been stripped. Simultaneously, Israel's public radio and television have prevented Arab leaders from voicing their claims and grievances by ceasing to interview them and, in this way, have intensified the alienation felt by their constituency.

As the new placards suggest, Arab citizens themselves are also under constant attack, particularly by right wing Jewish politicians who have been exploiting the pervasive fear to foment a form of fervent nationalism informed by racism. Effi Eitam, the new leader of the National Religious Party, who is a minister in Sharon's government, has characterized all Palestinian citizens of Israel as "a cancer," as if they were a tumor that needed to be rooted out. "Arabs," he claims, "will never have political rule in the country—not sovereignty, not an army, not any part, grain, or alleyway of the Land of Israel," which in Eitam's opinion includes the West Bank and Gaza Strip. His views have now been legitimized and have a following within the Jewish population.

It is within this stifling atmosphere that one must understand the slow resurgence of the Israeli peace camp. A number of incidents that have occurred over the past six months suggest, however, that the nationalistic refrain is beginning to be fractured.

First, the issue of "war crimes" was discussed for the first time by the mainstream media following the destruction of more than 50 houses in Rafah on January 10, which rendered at least 500 people homeless overnight in the midst of a cold winter—300 of whom are children. Along the same lines, the April assault on Jenin and the fiasco surrounding the aborted United Nations investigation team has also raised the issue of war crimes, and the possibility that Israeli officers could be arrested if they happen to visit European countries. There was a small rupture in the media, and a number of interviews and articles have appeared suggesting that soldiers should disobey commands that call upon them to commit illegal actions.

The second and probably most significant form of resistance was spurred by fifty combat officers and soldiers, who announced, in an open letter published on January 25 in the Israeli press, that they would no longer serve in the occupied territories. These reserve soldiers, among them many sergeants, lieutenants, captains, and even a few colonels, have organized a new movement called Courage to Refuse, which now comprises almost 500 members. Together with Yesh Gvul ("There Is a Limit"), the old conscientious-objector movement that was established during the Lebanon War, the refusenik community now has over 1,000 members.

Thousands of Israelis have called a telephone hotline to support the soldiers and to donate money to help them publish ads in local papers. A group of women has organized a petition, claiming that reservist men are not the only ones carrying the burdens of occupation, while there are close to 100 twelfth graders who have also announced that they will not serve in the occupied territories following their conscription this coming summer.

The uniqueness and force of the combat soldiers' letter, and the fact that it has created such a stir both inside the military establishment and society at large, has to do with the profile of the people who initiated it. These are not radical leftists but rather young men who are affiliated with Israel's political center; they are members of the social elite who characterize themselves as having been "raised upon the principles of Zionism, sacrifice and giving . . . who have always served in the front lines, and who were the first to carry out any mission, light or heavy, in order to protect the State of Israel and strengthen it." Moreover, they experienced firsthand the effect of the occupation, and no one can tell them that they don't know what is happening in the territories.

Finally, Israel is experiencing an economic crisis, with an official unemployment rate of close to 10 percent and negative growth expected for the year 2002. While this information has yet to be adequately used in order to criticize the occupation, more and more studies are appearing showing the disproportional amount of funding allocated to Jewish settlers in the West Bank and Gaza Strip and the detrimental effect of war spending on the economy, particularly the growing number of people who are living under the poverty line due to cuts in welfare benefits. Despite these and other pockets of resistance to Sharon's policies, it seems that darker times are lurking around the corner. The Bush administration has extended its unequivocal support of the Sharon government, thus allowing the Israeli security forces not only to strike the Palestinian Authority but also to silence all opposition from within. The crucial point that many foreigners neglect to notice is that in Israel, democracy is also under attack.

May 1, 2002

14

THE WAR LOOKS DIFFERENT ABROAD

Aviv Lavie

AT THE HEIGHT of the newspaper wiretapping scandal, when the pages of the two daily tabloids were turned into a battlefield of insults and distortions lacking any basic journalistic standards, there were those who proposed that the only way to save the newspapers' honor would be to leave the reporting in the hands of outside news agencies.* Lately, it appears to be time to raise the idea again—for coverage of the Israeli-Palestinian conflict.

A journey through the television and radio channels and the pages of the newspapers exposes a huge and embarrassing gap between what is reported to us and what is seen, heard, and read in the world—not only in the commentaries and analytical pieces, but also in the reporting of the dry facts.

Israel looks like an isolated media island, with most of the reporters drafted into the cause of convincing themselves and the reader that the government and army are perfectly justified in whatever they do. Some have actually been drafted—*Yediot Ahronot* has started running a regular column by its reporter, Guy Leshem, who reports with determination from the heart of the West Bank, straight from his military reserve

---

* The editors of *Ma'ariv* and *Yediot Ahronot*, Israel's two largest-circulation newspapers, were arrested in April 1995 for wiretapping each other—and more than 200 journalists, politicians, and businessmen—as part of a bid to increase circulation.

service. This is another step in erasing the line between the defense framework and the editorial framework that is supposed to report and criticize.

An Israeli citizen interested in a more complex picture of reality has to rely on the remote control and the computer mouse. "I've been here many years but I don't remember such a dark period in the Israeli press," complained one foreign correspondent, who indeed has been here many years. But even if he slightly exaggerated, it's not a totally unrealistic assessment.

The defense minister stuck to his word and absolutely prohibited sending Israeli reporters along with the army into Ramallah. The result: The Israeli media has no information about what is going on in the town.

Reporters and commentators get most of their information from the army, and a few also use Palestinian sources whom they regard with great suspicion. Many reporters believed the army was closed off to them for a few days, but as time goes by, they have been proven wrong. Since the journalists aren't on the ground to see firsthand, the soldiers become their eyes, which explains the huge difference between what is reported and broadcast to us, and what the rest of the world sees, particularly the Arab world.

On Arab television stations (though not only them) one could see Israeli soldiers taking over hospitals, breaking equipment, damaging medicines, and locking doctors away from their patients. In one interview, a doctor was whispering on a phone, explaining that he had to lower his voice lest the soldier in the next room cut off the conversation. Foreign television networks all over the world have shown the images of five Palestinians from the national security forces, shot in the head at close range; one was apparently the manager of the Palestinian Authority orchestra. Some of the networks have claimed they were shot in cold blood after they were disarmed.

The entire world has seen wounded people in the streets, heard reports of how the IDF prevents ambulances from reaching the wounded for treatment. The entire world has heard Palestinian residents saying they can't leave their homes because "they shoot anyone in the streets."

The entire world has heard testimony by Palestinian families who have been imprisoned in their homes for seventy-two hours, in some places without electricity or water, and the food is running out. There are also reports of vandalism and looting.

Maybe it's all mendacious propaganda (though in some cases, the pictures speak for themselves), but Israeli journalists have no way to investigate to find out the truth, whether to deflate the stories or confirm them. In the absence of that kind of reporting, instead, over and over, we hear the worn-out mantras about how "the civilian population is not our enemy," and reports on how the army takes such strict care not to harm civilians.

Israelis love to compare the American hunt for Osama bin Laden in the mountains of Afghanistan to the Israeli-Palestinian conflict. At least on one level, Israel indeed managed to create a parallel: Since Thursday night, the IDF has created an Afghanization of the Ramallah area. First, the Israeli media was neutralized, and then the IDF spokesman "recommended" to the foreign press that it leave the city, making clear that those who remained would be doing so at their own risk. Some reporters feel the IDF has opened war against them, not Yasser Arafat.

On Saturday, a TV France 2 team tried to reach Ramallah. At first they tried going through Psagot, and they ended up at the Qalandiyah checkpoint. When they were forbidden to pass, they pulled out their equipment to photograph the checkpoint, just so there would be something to show. It's allowed. But one of the soldiers—a reservist, according to the crew—ordered them to stop. They told him that he had no right to prevent them from filming and asked him to produce a written order from the Central Command that proved the area had been designated a closed military area. He had no such order. Instead, he began shouting at them and throwing things at them. Finally, when they turned their backs and began to go back to their car, a bullet sliced through the air between the cameraman and the reporter, Shaul Anderline.

Anderline is an Israeli citizen, who has lived here many years. In the wake of the incident he sent a vehement complaint to the IDF spokesman. The IDF spokesman said the "affair is being investigated."

Unofficially, IDF officers regard the incident as serious. In the last few days, two journalists have been shot in Ramallah, joining a growing list of reporters who have been wounded since the intifada broke out. The intentional shooting at Qalandiyah weakens the Israeli argument that the reporters were accidentally shot.

Journalists are also civilians, and in these days of blood, when the stomach turns and emotions work overtime, it influences even those whose profession requires them to be cool-headed and clear-minded. Unfortunately, those who want to find a model for just the opposite can turn to Friday's *Ma'ariv* headline: "With a Mighty Fist and an Out-stretched Arm" (quoting the Pesach Seder's evocation of God smiting the Egyptians). That headline writer can look to some of the American tabloid press, which right after the Twin Towers attack ran headlines like "Wanted Dead or Alive" over pictures of bin Laden (sometimes with the "Alive" crossed out).

Both in New York and Tel Aviv, when journalists cease collecting facts and asking questions, and instead turn to beating the war drums—yesterday, *Ma'ariv* editor Amnon Dankner ran a front-page article devoted to smashing, killing, trampling, and destroying—it's time to say good-bye, at least in the meantime, to a free press.

After the war, in a week or two, or a month, or maybe much longer, reporters will have to confront the things they wrote and said. Or maybe they won't. The archives are full of dusty folders full of the articles that appeared before the Yom Kippur War, and those extolling the consensus around the invasion of Lebanon. Nobody has yet really paid for what was written then, and already a new bill is mounting.

April 3, 2002

15

BREAK THE MIRROR NOW

Ilan Pappé

THE RECENT EVENTS in Palestine take us back to distant and more recent destinations. The strongest sense is the recurrence of the 1948 catastrophe, the *nakba*. More than fifty years on, there is a sense that the future of Mandatory Palestine was not as yet decided, and that its future was to be determined by force and not by negotiations. In 2002, the question has different geographical dimensions. The focus is on who will control the twenty-two percent of Palestine that did not become part of the State of Israel in 1948. Israel in 1948 was built on fifty-six percent of Palestine allocated to it by the UN, and an additional twenty-two percent occupied by force. Most of the roughly 900,000 Palestinians living in the newly formed state were expelled by force, their villages destroyed and their city neighborhoods settled by Jewish immigrants. Israel's creation was thus enabled by military power, ethnic cleansing and the de-Arabization of the country.

Since 1967, and more so since 1987, the future of the remaining twenty-two percent is the main issue on the local, and to some extent regional, agenda. Until 1993, the various Israeli governments wished to keep all the area under their full control, short of formal annexation, while expanding Jewish colonization and executing a policy of slow transfer. Any popular or armed resistance was brutally squashed, and yet the first intifada led the Israeli government in 1993 to be content with direct control over only part of the twenty-two percent, while allowing for the creation of a bantustan in the rest. This map, together with a demand to forgo the Palestinian right of return, was presented as a dictate to Arafat in Camp David in the summer of 2000. His refusal and a chain of by now known events led to the outbreak of the second intifada.

The margin between what Arafat was offered in Camp David and the vision of Ariel Sharon in 2002 is very narrow. The difference is in the number of square kilometers to be allocated to the bantustan, but the same principle guides both former generals. That principle is a Palestinian political entity devoid of any significant sovereignty and independence, with an "end of conflict" situation in which the Palestinians give up their right of return and aspirations for a capital in East Jerusalem. Sharon is not alone; he has the full support of the Israeli Labor Party, not only in his vision of the future but also in the tactics he employs to reach his goals. By his war against the Palestinian Authority and the creation of what he calls "security zones," Sharon wants to impose by force a new map on Palestine and Israel. Such a map should ensure, as the Zionists hoped in 1948, Israeli control over as great an area as possible with as few Palestinians as possible. Massive jailing, transfer, and intimidation were and will be used to redraw the map of Israel. Double-talk and avoiding any real chance at negotiations, in the few lulls in the fighting that opened such opportunities, are also part of the same strategy.

This is where the second, more recent, déjà vu, that of Lebanon in 1982, appears. It was the same Sharon, believing then as now that it is within his power to impose new political realities. He wanted to create a "new Lebanon." Today he thinks he has the power to create a new Israel and Palestine by moving a population, killing thousands and Judaizing additional parts of Palestine.

But history's repetitions are sometimes worse than the original events and less acceptable instances of human folly and cruelty. Israel's power and the power it is willing to employ are far more destructive than in the past. The systems that mobilize public opinion inside the Jewish state are far more sophisticated and effective than in the past; hence, the voices of dissent are fewer and weaker.

America is still behind Israel, as it was in 1948 and 1982, but at least part of Europe is not. The Arab world is committed, but as in the past mostly in word and not in deed. The Palestinians are alone against a powerful enemy poised to destroy them, as in the past. Israel's means vary with time, but the intention is still there. Many Jews in Israel, nonetheless, still adhere to noble aspirations such as the wish to build a democracy, maintain a very modernized economy and spread the wonders of Jewish and Hebraic culture and existence. But all these aspirations are dwarfed, indeed defeated, by the decision to sustain every achievement at the expense of the indigenous population of Palestine, whatever the price.

Other states opting for a similar policy and strategy would have been defined as pariah states long ago. But a European guilt complex (understandable, given the horrors of the Holocaust) and a strong Jewish lobby in the United States have thus far absolved politicians like Sharon from facing a fate similar to that of Slobodan Milosevic.

In the past two weeks Israel's amazing immunity has led some elements in global civil society to question its extraordinary status for the first time—even while Israel's war on media coverage of the army's actions in the West Bank still dissimulated the full extent of the havoc.

Despite the attempted cover-up, some basic facts have emerged about the IDF's actions and Sharon's strategy. The Israeli army is poised to destroy not only the Palestinian Authority, but also the infrastructure for independent, or even autonomous, Palestinian existence in the West Bank. If it succeeds, it will create a vacuum Sharon wants to fill with a mixture of two old Israeli notions of how to "rule" Arab areas: Israeli officers who will control life in areas deemed crucial by Israel, and a network of collaborators, modeled on the Village Leagues Sharon tried to establish in vain in 1981 as a substitute for the PLO. Such a new regime can be imposed in one of two ways: Either Sharon will reach an agreement with a local Palestinian leadership, sponsored by some Arab states, Europe and the United States; or, more likely, force will be used again, but more subtly, to "dilute" (borrowing from Israel's inhuman and dehumanized new political dictionary for a moment) the West Bank population. With whatever means the government finds, it will "encourage" Palestinians to move to Gaza and Jordan.

Sharon has about ten ministers in his government who endorse the plan openly, and a few in the Labor Party who implicitly take similar positions. As the next Israeli general elections approach, the Labor Party may leave the government, only to return afterward as a member of yet another unity government. But this should not blind us to the responsibility the Labor Party leaders share for the destruction of the Palestinian social, economic, and political infrastructure in the West Bank, and maybe later in the Gaza Strip. This destruction has been accompanied by humiliating acts and human rights abuses on a massive collective scale, as well as on a very symbolic level, toward Palestinian leaders—up to the top, to President Arafat. Massacres and physical destruction of houses and roads, too, are all part of a punitive mission disguised as a "war on terrorism."

Very few in Israel seek alternative interpretations of the "war on terrorism." Shocked by the human bombs that have produced a sense of personal insecurity and a rising death toll, the Israeli public in general is unable and unwilling to look through the catastrophic plans of the man they have elected democratically by an unprecedented majority. His posturing also caters to the dormant racist and ethnocentric attitudes of the vast majority of Jews, nurtured over the years by Israel's educational and cultural systems.

A coalition of groups opposing the war is trying to offer an alternative explanation to the bombs exploding in Israel and to the general Israeli policy. This coalition is made up of two blocs. The major one, led by Peace Now, has very little chance of providing a significant alternative. It is genuinely convinced that Barak made the most generous offer possible to the Palestinian side and that Arafat disappointed them. Their most common attitude is that "notwithstanding Arafat's unforgivable conduct, we have no other option but to conclude peace with this awful man." What they have in store is, again, the equation Barak made between Israeli withdrawal and peace. They never clarified to themselves or to the Jewish public what "peace" entails. As far as one can tell, it does not involve a solution to the refugee problem, a change in the status of the one-million-strong Palestinian minority in Israel (on whose vast support Peace Now relies for its demonstrations) or full sovereignty for the future Palestinian state. The evils of occupation are recognized, but mainly as corrupting Jewish society, not as crimes against the local population, and definitely not as a continuous evil that began with the ethnic cleansing of 1948.

Still, this is the only coalition capable of organizing massive demonstrations that elicit outside pressure on Israel to end its military operations, and one should not underestimate the urgency of such a development; but I doubt its ability to produce the change in Jewish public opinion necessary to open the way for peace and reconciliation. This element within the anti-war coalition widens the margins of public debate in Israel at a time when the media have silenced debate or reports that question the government's policies. Even so, these margins remain narrow as far as the attitude to the Palestinians, their plight, and rights are concerned.

The smaller group in this coalition is not even legitimized by the major component. It is centered around non-Zionist Jewish organizations and most of the Israeli-Palestinian parties. It offers a genuine alternative explanation and a way forward. But it is marginalized and fought not only by the establishment but also by the major component in the new peace and anti-war coalition. Its importance lies in its contacts with regional and global organizations that can empower both local and external action against occupation and in support of peace. This small component in the Israeli public space, as long as it is not totally silenced, can underline the wider set of issues that construct the oppressive nature of Zionism and Israel: the apartheid characteristics of policies toward Israel's Palestinian minority, the historical context of Israeli actions against the Palestinians in the occupied territories and Jewish society's need to acknowledge, then reconcile with, the crimes committed from the ethnic cleansing of 1948 until the "Defensive Shield" of today. That name is reminiscent of "Peace in Galilee," Israel's 1982 operation in Lebanon: two euphemisms for two destructive wars.

On a more personal note, I would add another déjà vu. As in 1993, during the heyday of Oslo, today the same despairing frustration about the future seeps in. I argued then, as I argue today, that even Peace Now is part of a single Zionist outlook, which does not allow recognition of past evils or of the need for genuine reconciliation with the Palestinian victims of Zionism and Israel. I am convinced today, as I was convinced then, that a far more fundamental and structural change has to occur in Jewish society for that to happen. Ten years ago, I pointed out apprehensively that we could not afford to let another decade pass, for more tragedies were in store. Now the sense that there is no time for long-term transformation is even more acute. We are running out of time, for the dangers of transfer and even genocide are hovering above us. Strong international intervention and pressure are necessary, so that the Israeli state and Jewish society alike may understand the moral and political price they will have to pay.

People abroad, reading what I—and my friends with similar views—write, think mistakenly that we scribble these analyses and predictions easily. In fact, a very long process of hesitation, deliberation and articulation took place before these positions were formulated. Our views place us in a very precarious position in our society. We are treated as insane at best, and at worst as traitors, even by those who claim to uphold the values of free speech and opinion in Israel. I am analyzing such a posture not from the point of view of risk or retribution, but rather from that of effectiveness: How can people like myself, so alienated by their own society and so revolted by what it and its government are doing, be effective in changing local public opinion? It sounds like a quixotic exercise. But then I remember all the Jews who joined the ANC, the civil rights movement in the United States and the anti-colonialist movement in France. I remember the brave Italians and Spaniards who did not succumb to the lure of fascism, and I draw courage from all these examples to go on telling my own people, from within, to break the mirror that shows them a superior moral body. They must replace it with one that exposes the crimes they, or on their behalf their various leaders and governments, are committing against humanity and the Palestinian people.

April 11, 2002

16

AFTER JENIN

Yitzhak Laor

WHAT HAS THE war between us and the Palestinians been about? About the Israeli attempt to slice what's left of Palestine into four cantons, by building "separation roads," new settlements, and checkpoints. The rest is killing, terror, curfew, house demolitions, and propaganda. Palestinian children live in fear and despair, their parents humiliated in front of them. Palestinian society is being dismantled, and public opinion in the West blames the victims—always the easiest way to face the horror. I know: My father was a German Jew.

Disastrously, the Israel Defense Forces are the country's imago. In the eyes of most Israelis, the IDF is pure, stainless; worse, it is seen as being above any political interest. Yet, like every army, it wants war, at least every once in a while. But whereas in other countries military power is balanced by civil society's institutions or by parts of the state itself (industry, banks, political parties, etc.), we in Israel have no such balance. The IDF has no real rival within the state, not even when the army's policy costs us our own lives (the lives of Palestinians, not to mention their welfare or dignity, are excluded from political discourse). There's no doubt that Israel's assassination policy—its killing of senior politicians (Dr. Thabet Thabet from Tulkarm, Abu Ali Mustafa from Ramallah) or of "terrorists" (sometimes labeled as such only after being eliminated)—has poured petrol on the fire. People talk about it, yet no politician from the right, the center, or even from the declining Zionist left has dared speak out against it. And despite critical articles in the press, the army has kept on doing what it wanted to do. Now they have had what they were really aiming for: an all-out attack on the West Bank.

Since September 11 the words "war against terror" have been popular, which is why everything Israel does is a war against terror, including the looting of the Khalil Sakakini Cultural Center in Ramallah. I'm against terror, too. I don't want to die walking my son to the mall. In fact I don't take him there anymore. I don't ride buses, and I'm scared that my family's turn will come, but I know that they—that is, our generals—accept terrorist attacks as a "reasonable price to pay" to reach a solution. What is their solution? Peace—what else? Peace between the victorious Israelis and the defeated Palestinians.

The IDF's ruthlessness should be read against the background of its defeat in Lebanon, when it was driven out after long years of waging a dirty war. Southern Lebanon was burned and destroyed by artillery and an air force that no terrorist organization could fight against. Yet 300 partisans—should I call them "terrorists"?—drove us (that is, our army) out twice. First in 1985, back into what our army and press used to call our "Security Zone" (the foreign media called it "Israel's self-proclaimed security zone"); and then, two years ago, out of that same Security Zone. The generals who were beaten then are running the current war. They have lived that defeat every day. And now they can teach them—that is, the Arabs—a lesson. Our heroes, armed with planes, helicopters and tanks, can arrest hundreds of people, concentrate them in camps behind barbed wire, without blankets or shelter, exploit the confusion to demolish more houses, fell more trees, take away more livelihoods. The bulldozer, once a symbol of the building of a new country, has become a monster following the tanks, so that everybody can watch as another family's home, another future disappears.

Israelis look to punish anyone who undermines our image of ourselves as victims. Nobody is allowed to take this image from us, especially not in the context of the war with the Palestinians, who are waging a war on "our home"—that is, their "non-home."

When a cabinet minister from a former socialist republic compared

Yasser Arafat to Hitler, he was applauded. Why? Because this is the way the world should see us, rising from the ashes. This is why we love Claude Lanzmann's *Shoah* (and even more his disgusting film about the IDF) and *Schindler's List*. Tell us more about ourselves as victims, and how we must be forgiven for every atrocity we commit. As my friend Tanya Reinhart has written, "It seems that what we have internalized [of the memory of the Holocaust] is that any evil whose extent is smaller is acceptable."

But this "evil of the past" has a peculiar way of entering our present life. On January 25, 2002, two months before the IDF got its license to invade the West Bank, Amir Oren, a senior military commentator for *Ha'aretz,* quoted a senior officer:

> In order to prepare properly for the next campaign, one of the Israeli officers in the territories said not long ago that it is justified and in fact essential to learn from every possible source. If the mission is to seize a densely populated refugee camp, or take over the casbah in Nablus, and if the commander's obligation is to try to execute the mission without casualties on either side, then he must first analyze and internalize the lessons of earlier battles—even, however shocking it may sound, even how the German Army fought in the Warsaw Ghetto.

The officer indeed succeeded in shocking others, not least because he is not alone in taking this approach. Many of his comrades agree that in order to save Israelis now, it is right to make use of knowledge that originated in that terrible war, whose victims were their kin.

Israel may not have a colonial past but we do have our memory of evil. Does this explain why Israeli soldiers stamped ID numbers on Palestinian arms? Or why the most recent Holocaust Day drew a ridiculous comparison between those of us in the besieged Warsaw Ghetto and those of us surrounding the besieged Jenin refugee camp? The satisfaction over the "victory" in Jenin was part of this constant lie. Some twenty Israeli soldiers (most of them reservists) died in what was supposed to be a zero-casualty campaign, but the defenders of the camp were equipped only with rifles and explosives.

On the Israeli side, as usual, there were special units, moving from one alleyway to another, assisted by a drone which supplied sophisticated information to the commanders at the rear. When that didn't work, there was the shelling of the camp, then the deployment of U.S.-supplied Apache helicopters to destroy houses along with dozens (or hundreds) of inhabitants. Was it a massacre? Like everything else in our corrupted life, it comes down to the number of dead: ten dead Israelis are a massacre; fifty dead Palestinians are not enough to count.

The destruction of the camp, whether spontaneous or premeditated by Sharon and company, reflects the determination of senior officers to finish their military service with a real achievement: the elimination of the Palestinian national movement, under the guise of the war against terror. But terror won't be beaten that way; on the contrary, enslaving a nation, bringing it to its knees, simply doesn't work. It never did. The long siege of the Church of the Nativity in Bethlehem is proof that the words "Israeli generals" no longer refer to men capable of strategic thought, or anything like it. Israeli generals may have fought some complicated battles in 1967, 1973, or even 1982, but in Bethlehem they have surrounded 200 young Palestinians for more than three weeks and let the whole world see their stubbornness and senseless cruelty. How, you may ask, can a disobedient nation like Israel follow so foolish a high command?

Here's the beginning of an answer. As the corpses lay rotting in Jenin, and small children were running around looking for food or their missing parents, and the wounded were still bleeding to death, with the IDF preventing any relief or UN officials from entering the camp (what did they have to hide?), the Ministry of Education issued an instruction to all schools that children should bring in parcels for the soldiers. "The most important thing," the teacher of my seven-year-old son said, "is a letter for the soldiers." Hundreds of thousands of children wrote such letters when the war against a civilian population was at its most extreme, under the critical observation of the world media. Imagine the ideological commitment of those children in the future. This is just one aspect of our oppositionless society.

The Israeli *imaginaire* is constituted, before anything else, of the belief in Israeli supremacy. When there is a cruel suicide bombing in a hotel in Netanya, we will respond on a greater scale, with a terrorist attack on them, no matter if it inflicts death or hunger on two million people who have no connection with that act, no matter if it creates a thousand more martyrs willing to blow themselves up with their victims. The military logic behind this behavior says: "We have the power and we have to exercise it, otherwise our existence is in danger." But the only danger is the one facing the Palestinians. Gas chambers are not the only way to destroy a nation. It is enough to destroy its social tissue, to starve dozens of villages, to induce high rates of infant mortality. The West Bank is going through a Gaza-ization. Please don't shrug your shoulders. The one thing that might help to destroy the consensus in Israel is pressure from the West, on which the Israeli elite is dependent in so many ways.

April 22, 2002

Part Three

REFUSAL

17

SAYING NO TO ISRAEL'S OCCUPATION

Ishai Menuchin

IN THIS TIME of madness and carnage, hope for peace between Israel and the Palestinians appears impossible. After thirty-five years of Israel's occupation of the West Bank and Gaza, the two sides seem only to have grown accustomed to assassinations, bombings, terrorist attacks and house demolitions. Each side characterizes its own soldiers as either "defense forces" or "freedom fighters," when in truth these soldiers take part in war crimes on a daily basis. Daily funerals and thoughts of revenge among Israelis tend to blur the fact that we, the Israelis, are the occupiers. And as much as we live in fear of terrorism and war, it is the Palestinians who suffer more deaths hourly and live with greater fear because they are the occupied.

Twenty years ago, when I was first inducted into the Israeli Army to serve as a paratrooper and officer for four and a half years, I took an oath to defend Israel and obey my commanders. I was young, a patriot, probably naïve, and sure that as a soldier my job was to defend my home and country. It did not occur to me that I might be used to carry out an occupation or asked to fight in military engagements that are not essential for the defense of Israel.

It took me one war—the Lebanon war—many dead friends, and some periods of service in the occupied territories to find that my assumptions were wrong. In 1983, I refused to serve in acts of occupation, and I spent thirty-five days in military prison for my refusal. Today, as a major in the reserves of the Israel Defense Forces, I still defend my country, but I will not participate in a military occupation that has over the decades made Israel less secure and less humane. The escalating violence is evidence of this truth.

Being a citizen in a democracy carries with it a commitment to democratic values and a responsibility for your actions. It is morally impossible to be both a devoted democratic citizen and a regular offender against democratic values. Depriving people of the right to equality and freedom, and keeping them under occupation, is by definition an antidemocratic act. The occupation that has now lasted a generation and rules the lives of more than 3.5 million Palestinians is what drives me, hundreds of other objectors in the armed forces, and tens of thousands of Israeli citizens to oppose our government's policies and actions in the West Bank and Gaza.

My commitment to democratic values caused me to act against the occupation—to sign petitions, write ads, and take part in demonstrations and vigils. But those acts of opposition were not enough to absolve me of having to make a moral choice about participating in the occupation as an officer and ordering others to do so. So while I continue to serve in the Defense Forces, I selectively refuse military orders if they require my presence in the territories outside the pre-1967 Israeli borders. I will not obey illegal orders to execute potential terrorists or fire into civilian demonstrations. (Since October 2000 more than 850 Palestinians have been killed by my army: 178 were minors, and 55 were executed.) And I will not take part in "less violent" actions like keeping Palestinians under curfew for months, manning roadblocks that prevent civilians moving from town to town, or carrying out house demolitions and other acts of repression aimed at the entire Palestinian population.

As our government prepares to increase military action in the West Bank and Gaza, Israelis need a true debate about the nature of Israel's presence in these territories. Israeli and international human rights groups have raised their voices about the persistent violation of Palestinian human rights. I believe it is my duty as a citizen of a democratic nation to protest this conduct, which cannot be justified.

I and others who serve in the Israel Defense Forces cannot by our actions alone change government policies or make peace negotiations more likely. But we can show our fellow citizens that occupation of the territories is not just a political or strategic matter. It is also a moral matter. We can show them an alternative—they can say no to occupation. When we begin to see Israel's situation in that light, perhaps we will be able to let go of our fear enough to find a way forward.

March 9, 2002

18

RED LINE, GREEN LINE, BLACK FLAG
Yigal Shochat

THE TRUTH IS that I don't yet have a fully formed opinion on the subject of sweeping refusal to serve in the IDF. I am in favor of the state, in favor of preserving its security, in favor of defending the state within its borders, and also in favor of the war against the terrorism—local and international—that threatens Israel.

On the other hand, I cannot abide the naturalness with which the occupation is continuing; the fact that one generation after another of soldiers is serving the occupation and that these soldiers are the ones who effectively give the successive governments the power to hold on to the territories and the settlements and to suppress the Palestinian population. Therefore, I find myself on the horns of a large dilemma. In the meantime, I have resolved it, for myself, by deciding that I am in favor of refusal to serve in the territories but not refusal to serve altogether. I know that this is a somewhat hypocritical position, because sometimes the soldier who is posted at General Staff headquarters can do more injustice than a soldier at a roadblock.

Still, I think that refusing to serve in the occupied territories sends a sharper political and moral message. It says that you are ready to guard your country and fight for it, but that you are not willing to suppress another people indefinitely, when the security benefit for Israel is negative. In fact, serving in the occupied territories undermines the country's security while contributing to the security of the settlers. On that subject, I think we have across-the-board agreement by now.

In the case of pilots—pilots of warplanes, helicopter pilots, pilots in general—it makes no sense to talk about refusing to serve across the 1967 Green Line. Pilots do not serve at the place to which they are posted. In effect, they have to decide anew every day, and sometimes every hour, which operations are moral and legal and which are not. I am not naïve: I am well aware that any pilot who will refuse to bomb Nablus or Ramallah once or twice will thereby bring his career to an end—and we are talking about a career. To fly is a way of life and a profession. It is never just the draft and reserve duty, which you do in order to get it over with and get back home in one piece. So, in the case of pilots, I think we need to expand the concept of the "black flag."

In my opinion, pilots need to examine closely the order they get, ask a lot of questions about the goal, and refuse to obey an order they consider immoral. I am afraid that such questions do not occupy them; rather, they compete among themselves over who will be assigned the next mission to liquidate someone in the center of Nablus, on the main street, or who will get to drop a bomb on a building in Ramallah. They probably return to the squadron happy when they score a bull's-eye and are sorry, to some extent, if civilians are killed. I remember this from my own experience. People want to excel in what they do, and they want action. That's why they are pilots in the first place.

I think that F-16 pilots should refuse to bomb Palestinian cities. They have to think about what a bombing operation would be like in the city they live in. Let's say that Arafat were to decide to level the police station on Dizengoff Boulevard using a warplane. (Let's say he had a warplane.) If Arafat were to conclude that this is how he could convince Sharon to withdraw from the territories, would we accept a bombing operation in the center of the city as a legitimate military act? After all, we call even an operation against an IDF outpost, like the one last week at Kerem Shalom, a "terrorist" attack.*

I can imagine what it was like in Ramallah when an F-16 bombed the police station there. I am not talking about the civilians who were killed there—cooks from Gaza, not troops. I am talking about bombing a densely populated city. I am talking about liquidating people on the

---

* This January 9, 2002 attack by a Hamas unit in southern Gaza killed four Israeli soldiers.

main street, from a helicopter, with three passersby also killed. It's impossible today to say that this was "collateral damage," that we didn't intend to kill civilians, because when a plane bombs a populated city, you take into account that civilians could get killed. Even in precision bombing. So I view this as the deliberate killing of civilians—a war crime. We have seen in the past few months what smart bombs can do, both here and in Afghanistan.

I think that the goal is not important enough to pay that price, especially when we are confronting not an army but civilians. And more especially when we are wrong. Very wrong. In my view, neither the larger goal of this fighting is legitimate—because the occupation is not legitimate—nor the smaller goal of destroying a police station in order to pressure Arafat into stopping the use of terrorism. That, too, is not legitimate.

In 1996, I did not accept the legitimacy of Operation Grapes of Wrath, where the purpose was to force Lebanese civilians to flee by bombing them, thereby pressuring the government in Beirut to take action against Hizbollah.* But it is not only pilots who are responsible for war crimes. I think that, in the final analysis, the pilots may be less responsible than other soldiers. I think that every driver of an army bulldozer has to refuse to obey an order to demolish homes with the aim of exposing an area for the convenience of the IDF.

I read this week what the head of the Civil Administration, Brigadier General Dov Tzadka, said about the authorizations he gives to demolish houses and groves, and how the army then goes hyperactive and levels the area he authorized twice. By what right does he approve such an operation in the first place? I am constantly dumbfounded at how these people get up every morning and go to work: After all, we're not talking about kids of draft age, this is a brigadier general. What does he say to himself at the end of the day? "Today I authorized the uprooting of twelve and a half acres of strawberry fields"? What for? To preserve the country's security?

---

* One such attack at a UN compound near Qana on April 18, 1996 took the lives of more than 100 Lebanese civilians.

I saw that this Brigadier General Tzadka is now worried that he may end up at the war crimes tribunal in The Hague, because he knows full well what he did. But how can you both know and do? I think that to demolish civilian homes only because they are obstructing someone's field of vision constitutes a flagrantly immoral military act. I am not a legal expert, and so I don't know what is legal and what isn't, but I assume that this is illegal as well as immoral. I know that the question of when the black flag flies over an order is a wholly personal one. One can't wait for the court to declare a certain operation flagrantly illegal, nor should one wait, because then it becomes a retroactive matter, as in the case of Ehud Yatom [who, according to the High Court of Justice, took part in the killing of two captured terrorists at the order of the head of the Shin Bet security service in 1984].

There are some people who never see a black flag, not even when it involves the murder of an Arab who is bound. There are people who only see a black flag when they get old, like me, because when I was a young pilot, I wasn't selective. I did what I was told to do. I am in favor of a broader use of the concept of the black flag, which means to refuse to obey an order that in your personal opinion is flagrantly illegal. But I know that draft-age soldiers, and even people in the career army, will not make much use of it. When you're inside, you see things differently.

I think also that to stand at a roadblock and make a selection as to who will be allowed to proceed to a hospital or to a maternity ward and who will not is also flagrantly illegal. Therefore, I think that every soldier who is assigned to serve at a roadblock should refuse the order and instead go to prison. If only the legality of the selection process at roadblocks were examined in court. I think that those who refuse to serve in the territories should not make do with going to jail; they should try to reach civil courts so that these things will be reviewed and given publicity. Let them go all the way to the High Court of Justice with their refusal. Those who go to jail quietly do not exert an influence.

It is out of the question to allow the army to set up roadblocks at every corner that prevent people from going about their lives, going to work, going to the doctor, and to accept this as though it is a divine decree. That constitutes collective punishment of civilians, which is illegal according to the Geneva Conventions. I think that it's a shame that so few people refuse to serve in the territories, but I can't really complain, because I didn't do it either when I should have done it.

Nearly twenty years ago, I paid a visit to the late Professor Yeshayahu Leibowitz. He asked me then—this was in 1983—how it was possible that there weren't 500 officers who would refuse to serve in the territories. He said that in his opinion, if there were 500 officers like that, the occupation would end immediately. I think he was right. Soon we will not be able to refer to an "occupation," because being present on the ground for so many years creates a new situation.

People who served in the territories in their compulsory service return as reservists, and their children are also stationed in the same places. The new generation doesn't even know the Palestinians because of the lengthy closure, and to them, the territories are like Lebanon. Apartheid against the Palestinians is practiced by one generation to the next. And not only by the settlers—by all of us. If there are no terrorist attacks, we don't even remember that the Palestinians exist.

I don't know whether every operation I took part in when I was an active fighter pilot was legal or moral. Probably not. Today, friends from that period who bombed targets with me complain to me that I remembered too late to be a bleeding heart and that it's no big deal to talk about refusal to obey orders when I am no longer involved and I will not be the one to go to jail. They say that as long as my promotion in the army was at stake I said nothing, but now that I have nothing to lose I am suddenly a hero. That is all true. I reached political and moral maturity very late.

But I can also say, roughly, that I always bombed military targets. When I bombed civilian neighborhoods, it was during a full-scale war, when planes and tanks and soldiers from both sides were locked in combat, and it was far from sure who would win. In general, in the wars in which I took part, our feeling was that Israel was in an inferior position and that we were fighting for our lives and our home, literally. As to the territories, as to this military struggle against the Palestinians, I simply don't see armies facing off and I don't see a war. In fact, I don't even know which side of the fence I'm on, because I am certainly not on the side of the settlers. What I see is an occupied population that has a few hundred rifles and mortars, which is trying to expel us, while we refuse to go because we have invested a few cents in unnecessary settlements.

I am aware of the arguments against refusal. First of all, they say that in a democracy, it is the role of the elected political level to decide what constitutes a legitimate goal and what does not. I reject that. Precisely in a democracy, it is the right and the duty of every citizen to oppose illegitimate warfare. In totalitarian regimes, people who refuse to serve are shot, while here they are only sent to prison briefly. It is in a democracy that you have the option of not following the herd.

The second argument is that we need more humanists at the roadblocks in order to ease things for the Palestinians and that we must not leave the army to the nutcases on the right. I also deny the importance that is attributed to individual soldiers at a roadblock, because in the course of time, they all become insensitive to suffering. I think that the individual soldier carries the greatest weight when he refuses to serve.

The third argument is that if everyone were to decide which orders to obey, the time would come when the settlers would refuse to evacuate the settlements. To that I say: That's fine with me. For my part, the settlers can refuse to evacuate the settlements and we will do it for them. I, for example, would refuse to demolish the home of a Palestinian with a bulldozer, and at the same time, some soldier-settler would refuse to evacuate a settler family. That's fine with me. The important thing is for soldiers to retain their humanity and realize that they are confronting dilemmas.

In my opinion, all the IDF's operations in the territories are approaching the red line of the black flag. I cannot judge what is legal and what constitutes a war crime. At a time when the Americans kill thousands of people in an attempt to find one person, it is difficult to talk about morality in war. Since the establishment of the Palestinian Authority, following the Oslo accords, we have begun to treat it as a state even though it is not. That makes it easier for us to attack it with weapons, such as planes and tanks, that are intended for use against armies in war. My feeling is that we have crossed a line, and I am afraid that the day is not far off when we will bomb the Arabs in Israel the way we opened fire on them in the demonstrations of October 2000.*

The day is not far off when the Israel Air Force will bomb Umm al-Fahm, in the same way that Saddam Hussein bombed his Kurdish citizens. I don't know if the Air Force pilots will refuse to obey such an order. There will be someone to persuade them that the operation is logical and essential, that the bombs are smart, that the only targets are city hall and the Islamic movement, and not innocent people. I don't see any great difference between that and bombing Ramallah.

January 20, 2002

* At the beginning of the intifada, Palestinian citizens of Israel organized unarmed demonstrations in solidarity with Palestinians in the territories, which the Israeli army suppressed by firing live ammunition at the protesters, killing thirteen. One scene of conflict was the predominantly Palestinian town of Umm al-Fahm, which is in northern Israel near the line separating Israel from the territories.

19

AN OPEN LETTER TO COLONEL AVIV KOHAVI, BRIGADE COMMANDER OF THE ISRAELI PARATROOPERS

Neve Gordon

Dear Aviv,

I presume you remember me. In any event, I remember you. We first met in the paratrooper brigade. I was a platoon sergeant in the corporals company; you were a young platoon officer. Even then friends of mine who were serving with you in the same post in Lebanon related that you were a sensible, serious, and above all decent officer.

The better part of our acquaintance occurred, though, at Hebrew University. We were studying toward our Bachelor of Arts in Philosophy—you in preparation for a career in the military, I as a human rights activist. During that period we had more than one political discussion. I couldn't help but admire you. I found you to be a thinking person, imaginative, and judicious—quite different from the typical army officer that one meets at the university, one who registers merely to snatch a degree and to run off. Looking back, I believe that you really enjoyed your studies, a number of which, it should be noted, dealt with ethical theory.

Years have passed since we last met. You became the paratroopers brigade commander, I a lecturer in the department of politics and government at Ben Gurion University. On Thursday, March 1, 2002, I saw you once again, not face-to-face, but on television. You were on the news program, the commander of the troops that entered Balata refugee camp, near Nablus. You solemnly explained that at that very moment your soldiers were transmitting a forceful message to the Palestinian terrorists: The Israeli army will hunt them down in every nook and cranny.

In the days after the interview, news began to trickle out about what took place in the camp: Prior to the incursion the Israeli military rained terror on the inhabitants, employing helicopters and tanks; then, Aviv, you imposed a curfew on the camp, blew up the electric transmission lines, cutting off electricity to 20,000 civilian inhabitants; bulldozers ruined the water supply pipelines. Your soldiers, Aviv, then moved from house to house by smashing holes in the interior walls; they destroyed furniture and other property, and riddled rooftop water tanks with bullets. The soldiers spread terror on the inhabitants, most of whom were women, elderly, and children.

But that wasn't all. I learned that your soldiers also used inhabitants as human shields. Also, that in the first few hours of the incursion the Palestinians had 120 wounded, and you, Aviv, refused to allow ambulances to enter or leave the camp.

There were, of course, several battles in the camp during the incursion; two Palestinians and one of your soldiers were killed. You also reported that you confiscated weapons and that your operation prevented future terrorist acts from happening. But you totally ignored the connection between Israeli military violence perpetrated in the occupied territories and Palestinian violence in Israel, as if the incursions into the camps and the reign of terror that you and your soldiers imposed do not drive Israel/Palestine into a bloodbath from which none can escape.

How, Aviv, do you think that your incursion affected the children whom you locked up for hours with other members of their families, while you searched their houses and blasted holes through their walls? Did the infiltration contribute a smithereen to peace, or did it instead spread seeds of hatred, despondence, and death in the crowded, poverty-stricken, hopeless refugee camp?

I have not stopped thinking about you since that television interview, trying to understand what was going on in your mind. What caused you to lead your soldiers—soldiers of the paratrooper brigade—to a war against a civilian population?

Aviv, I am presently teaching a course entitled "The Politics of Human Rights." One of the topics I discuss during the semester is the intifada and its lessons with respect to human rights. From the standpoint of international conventions, at least, your acts in Balata constitute blatant violations of human rights. Such acts are, in fact, war crimes.

Aviv, what happened to the sensible and judicious officer? How did you become a war criminal?

DR. NEVE GORDON
March 29, 2002

20

AN OPEN LETTER TO BENJAMIN BEN-ELIEZER, MINISTER OF DEFENSE

Sergio Yahni

An officer for whom you are responsible has sentenced me today to twenty-eight days in military prison for my refusal to serve in reserve duty. I did not refuse only to serve in the occupied Palestinian territories, as I have for the past fifteen years, I refused to serve in the Israeli army in any capacity.

Since September 29, 2000, the Israeli army has waged a "dirty war" against the Palestinian Authority. This dirty war includes extrajudicial killings, the murder of women and children, the destruction of the economic and social infrastructure of the Palestinian population, the burning of agricultural fields and the uprooting of trees. You have sowed fear and despair but failed to achieve your ultimate objective; the Palestinian people have not given up their dream of sovereignty and independence. Neither did you provide security for your own people, despite all the destructive violence of the army over which you have responsibility.

In light of your great failure, we are now witness to an intellectual debate amongst Israelis of the worst kind: a discussion about the possible deportation and the mass killing of Palestinians.

The failed attempt of leaders of the Labor Party to impose a settlement on the Palestinian people has dragged us into a "dirty war" for which Palestinians and Israelis are paying with their lives. The racist violence of the Israeli security establishment, who do not see people but only "terrorists," has deepened the vicious cycle of violence for both Palestinians and Israelis.

Israelis are also the victims of this war. They are the victims of the irresponsible and failed aggression of the army over which you are responsible. Even when you waged the most deadly attacks on the Palestinian people, you did not fulfill your duty: giving security to the citizens of Israel. Tanks in Ramallah cannot stop your most monstrous creation: the desperation which explodes in coffee shops. You, and the military officers under your command, have created human beings whose humanity disappears out of desperation and humiliation.

You have created this despair and you cannot stop it.

It is clear to me that you have risked all of our lives only in order to continue building illegal and immoral settlements, for Gush Etzion, Efrat and Kedumim: for the cancer which eats away at the Israeli social body. For the past thirty-five years, the settlements have turned the Israeli society into a danger zone. The Israeli state has sowed despair and death both for the Palestinians and Israelis.

Therefore I will not serve in your army. Your army, which calls itself the "Israel Defense Forces," is nothing more than the armed wing of the settlement movement. This army does not exist to bring security to the citizens of Israel, it exists to guarantee the continuation of the theft of Palestinian land. As a Jew, I am repelled by the crimes this militia commits against the Palestinian people.

It is both my Jewish and my human duty to resolutely refuse to take any part in this army. As the son of a people victim to pogroms and destruction, I cannot be a part of your insane policies. As a human being, it is my duty to refuse to participate in any institution which commits crimes against humanity.

SINCERELY,
SERGIO YAHNI
March 19, 2002

21

WHY?

Assaf Oron

ON FEBRUARY 5, 1985, I got up, left my home, went to the Compulsory Service Center on Rashi Street in Jerusalem, said good-bye to my parents, boarded the rickety old bus going to the Military Absorption Station and turned into a soldier.

Exactly seventeen years later, I find myself in a head-to-head confrontation with the army, while the public at large is jeering and mocking me from the sidelines. Right-wingers see me as a traitor who is dodging the holy war that's just around the corner. The political center shakes a finger at me self-righteously and lectures me about undermining democracy and politicizing the army. And the left? The square, establishment, "moderate" left that only yesterday was courting my vote now turns its back on me as well. Everyone blabbers about what is and what is not legitimate, exposing in the process the depth of their ignorance of political theory and their inability to distinguish a real democracy from a Third World regime in the style of Juan Perón. Almost no one asks the main question: Why would a regular guy get up one morning in the middle of life, work, the kids and decide he's not playing the game anymore? And how come he is not alone but there are fifty . . . I beg your pardon, a hundred . . . beg your pardon again, now almost two hundred regular, run-of-the-mill guys like him who've done the same thing?

Translated by Amichai Kronfeld

Our parents' generation lets out a sigh: We've embarrassed them yet again. But isn't it all your fault? What did you raise us on? On the one hand, universal ethics and universal justice; peace, liberty and equality to all. And on the other hand: "The Arabs want to throw us into the sea"; "They are all crafty and primitive—you can't trust them." On the one hand, the songs of John Lennon, Pete Seeger, Bob Dylan, Bob Marley, Pink Floyd. Songs of peace and love and against militarism and war. On the other hand, songs about a sweetheart riding the tank after sunset in the field: "The tank is yours and you are ours" [allusion to a popular Israeli folk song]. I was raised on two value systems: One was the ethical code and the other the tribal code, and I naïvely believed that the two could coexist.

This is the way I was when I was drafted. Not enthusiastic, but as if embarking on a sacred mission of courage and sacrifice for the benefit of society. But when, instead of a sacred mission, a nineteen-year-old finds himself performing the sacrilege of violating human beings' dignity and freedom, he doesn't dare ask—even himself—if it's OK or not. He simply acts like everyone else and tries to blend in. As it is, he's got enough problems, and boy is the weekend far off.

You get used to it in a hurry, and many even learn to like it. Where else can you go out on patrol—that is, walk the streets like a king, harass and humiliate pedestrians to your heart's content, and get into mischief with your buddies—and at the same time feel like a big hero defending your country? The Gaza Exploits became heroic tales, a source of pride for the Giv'ati brigade, then a relatively new brigade suffering from low self-esteem.

For a long time, I could not relate to the whole "heroism" thing. But when, as a sergeant, I found myself in charge, something cracked inside me. Without thinking, I turned into the perfect occupation enforcer. I settled accounts with "upstarts" who didn't show enough respect. I tore up the personal documents of men my father's age. I hit, harassed, served as a bad example—all in the city of Qalqilyah, barely three miles from grandma and grandpa's home-sweet-home. No. I was no "aberration." I was exactly the norm.

Having completed my compulsory service, I was discharged, and then the first intifada began (how many more await us?). Ofer, a comrade in arms who remained in the service, has become a hero: the hero of the second Giv'ati trial. He commanded a company that dragged a detained Palestinian demonstrator into a dark orange grove and beat him to death. As the verdict stated, Ofer was found to have been the leader in charge of the whole business. He spent two months in jail and was demoted—I think that was the most severe sentence given an Israeli soldier through the entire first intifada, in which about a thousand Palestinians were killed. Ofer's battalion commander testified that there was an order from the higher echelons to use beatings as a legitimate method of punishment, thereby implicating himself. On the other hand, Effi Eitam, the brigade commander, who had been seen beating Arabs on numerous occasions, denied that he ever gave such an order and consequently was never indicted. Today he lectures us on moral conduct on his way to a new life in politics.* (In the current intifada, incidentally, the vast majority of incidents involving Palestinian deaths are not even investigated. No one even bothers.) And in the meantime, I was becoming more of a civilian. A copy of *The Yellow Wind* [a 1988 book on life in the occupied territories by David Grossman], which had just come out, crossed my path. I read it, and suddenly it hit me. I finally understood what I had done over there. What I had *been* over there.

I began to see that they had cheated me: They raised me to believe there was someone up there taking care of things. Someone who knows stuff that is beyond me, the little guy. And that even if sometimes politicians let us down, the "military echelon" is always on guard, day and night, keeping us safe, each and every one of their decisions the result of sacred necessity. Yes, they cheated us, the soldiers of the intifadas, exactly as they had cheated the generation that was beaten to a pulp in the War of Attrition and in the Yom Kippur War, exactly as they had cheated the generation that sank deep into the Lebanese mud during the Lebanon invasions. And our parents' generation continues to be silent. In a painful process that took several years, I finally understood that I was raised on two contradictory value systems. I think most people discover even at an earlier age they must choose between two value systems: an abstract, de-

* Eitam now leads the National Religious Party and serves in Ariel Sharon's cabinet.

manding one that is no fun at all and that is very difficult to verify, and another that calls to you from every corner—determining who is up and who is down, who is king and who is pariah, who is one of us and who is our enemy. Contrary to basic common sense, and hesitatingly at first, I picked the first system. Comparing the profitability of these two systems in our country, I cannot blame those who choose the second.

I found myself volunteering in a small, smoke-filled office in East Jerusalem, digging up files about deaths, brutality, bureaucratic viciousness or simple daily harassment. I felt I was atoning, to some extent, for my actions during my days with the Giv'ati brigade. But it also felt as if I was trying to empty the ocean out with a teaspoon.

Out of the blue, I was called up for the very first time for reserve duty in the occupied territories. Hysterically, I contacted my company commander. He calmed me down: We will be staying at an outpost overlooking the Jordan River. No contacts with the local population are expected. And that indeed was what I did, but some of my friends provided security for the Damia Bridge terminal [where Palestinians cross from Jordan to Israel and vice versa]. This was in the days preceding the Gulf War, and a large number of Palestinian refugees were flowing from Kuwait to the occupied territories (out of the frying pan, into the fire). The reserve soldiers—mostly right-wingers—cringed when they saw the female conscripts stationed in the terminal happily ripping open down comforters and babies' coats to make sure they didn't contain explosives. They tried to stop them, but couldn't. I too cringed when I heard their stories, but I was also hopeful: Reserve soldiers are human after all, whatever their political views.

Such hopes were dashed three years later, when I spent three weeks with a celebrated reconnaissance company in the confiscated ruins of a villa at the outskirts of the Abasans [in Gaza]. This is where it became clear to me that the same humane reserve soldier could also be an ugly, wretched, macho man regressing back to his days as a young conscript. Already on the bus ride to the Gaza Strip, the soldiers were competing to see whose "heroic" tales of murderous beatings during the intifada were better (in case you missed this point, the beatings were literally murderous: beating *to death*). Going on patrol duty with these guys once was all that I could take. I went up to the placement officer and requested to be given guard duty only. Placement officers like people like me: most soldiers can't tolerate staying inside the base for longer than a couple of hours. Two newfound friends with a similar oddity kept me company.

Thus began the nausea and shame routine, which lasted three tours of reserve duty in the occupied territories during 1993, 1995, and 1997. The "pale-gray" refusal routine. For several weeks at a time I would turn into a hidden "prisoner of conscience," guarding an outpost or a godforsaken transmitter on top of some mountain, a recluse. I was ashamed to tell most of my friends why I chose to serve this way. I didn't have the energy to hear them get on my case for being such a "bleeding heart." I was also ashamed of myself. This was the easy way out. In short, I was ashamed all over. I did "save my own soul." I was not directly engaged in wrongdoing—I only made it possible for others to do so while I kept guard. Why didn't I refuse outright? I don't know. It was partly the pressure to conform, partly the political process that gave us a glimmer of hope that the whole occupation business would be over soon. More than anything, it was my curiosity to see actually what was going on over there.

And precisely because I knew so well, firsthand from years of experience, what was going on over there, what reality was like over there, I had no trouble seeing through the fog of war and the curtain of lies what has been taking place since the earliest days of the second intifada. For years, the army had been feeding on lines like "We were too nice in the first intifada," and "If we had only killed a hundred in the very first days, everything would have been different." Now the army was given license to do things its way. I knew full well that Ehud Barak was giving the army a free hand, and that Shaul Mofaz was taking full advantage of this to maximize the bloodshed.

By then, I had two little kids, boys, and I knew from experience that no one—not a single person in the entire world—will ever make sure that my sons won't have to serve in the occupied territories when they reach eighteen. No one, that is, except me. And no one but me will have to look them in the eye when they're all grown up and tell them where dad was when all that happened. It was clear to me: This time I was not going.

Initially, this was a quiet decision, still a little shy, something like "I am just a bit weird, can't go and can't talk about it too much either." But as time went by, as the level of insanity, hatred, and incitement kept rising, as the generals were turning the Israel Defense Forces into a terror organization, the decision was turning into an outcry: "If you can't see that this is one big crime leading us to the brink of annihilation, then something is terribly wrong with you!"

And then I discovered that I was not alone. Like discovering life on another planet. The truth is that I understand why everyone is mad at us. We spoiled the neat little order of things. The holy status quo states that the right holds the exclusive rights to celebrate the blood and ask for more. The role of the left, on the other hand, is to wail while sitting in their armchairs sipping wine and waiting for the Messiah to come and with a single wave of his magic wand make the right disappear along with the settlers, the Arabs, the weather, and the entire Middle East. That's how the world is supposed to work. So why are you causing such a disturbance? What's your problem? Bad boys! Woe to you, dear establishment left! You haven't been paying attention! That Messiah has been here already. He waved his magic wand, saw things aren't that simple, was abandoned in the midst of battle, lost altitude, and finally was assassinated, with the rest of us (yes, me too) watching from the comfort of our armchairs. Forget it. A messiah doesn't come around twice! There is no such thing as a free lunch.

Don't you really see what we are doing, why it is that we stepped out of line? Don't you get the difference between a low-key, personal refusal and an organized, public one? (And make no mistake about it, the private refusal is the easier choice.) You really don't get it? So let me spell it out for you.

First, we declare our commitment to the first value system. The one that is elusive, abstract, and not profitable. We believe in the moral code generally known as God (and my atheist friends who also signed this letter will have to forgive me—we all believe in God, the true one, not that of the rabbis and the ayatollahs). We want to remind you all that there is such a moral code above and inside each and every one of you. We believe that our tribal code has strayed too far, and now it has become nothing more than idolatry in disguise. *There is no room for cooperation with this idolatry.* Those who let such a form of idol worship take over will end up as burnt offerings themselves.

Second, we (as well as some other groups who are even more despised and harassed) are trying—with our bare hands—to stop the next war. The most pointless, idiotic, cruel, and immoral war in the history of Israel.

We are the young Chinese man standing in front of the tank. And you? If you are nowhere to be seen, you are probably inside the tank, advising the driver.

February 6, 2002

RULING OVER A HOSTILE POPULATION
Shamai Leibowitz

OUR RULE OVER three million Palestinian Arabs in the territories has perforce put us in a position of committing a number of moral outrages. Continued rule will necessitate not only continued denial of many basic rights to Palestinians but will require our taking additional steps that are reprehensible, if not morally questionable. While we certainly did not set out intentionally to take drastic measures to buttress our rule, these are willy-nilly consequences of such a position. To maintain our rule we will have to continue to mete out collective punishment that often cruelly affects those who are not guilty.

Among the steps we have taken is the enclosing of millions of humans in their cities, towns, and villages. We often deny basic rights, such as the right to earn a living, to study, to move freely, to purchase basic necessities, to vote, to travel for medical care, to move sick or injured to medical facilities, etc. But most severe is that innocent civilians die. While this occurs in every violent conflict throughout the world, and throughout history, what is happening now is more than unintentional collateral deaths of civilians. Ruling over millions of people who despise your rule necessitates such deaths of youngsters, women, and elderly.

The IDF, like any army, makes both avoidable and unavoidable mis-

Translated by Cheryl Leibowitz-Schmidt

takes; but it is certainly not bloodthirsty and has no daily quota of corpses. It is not an oxymoron to term the IDF a humane army. Nevertheless, it seems that a large number of the hundreds of Palestinian civilians who die are killed not because Israeli armed forces are acting in self-defense. The IDF maintains that these are victims of unavoidable actions that must be taken to quell unrest. In this respect, the IDF is correct, because to put down a popular uprising drastic measures (i.e., maiming and killing civilians) are often needed, in addition to the enforcing of curfews, establishment of blockades, abrogation of civil rights, and condoning of inhumane treatment. The governmental decision to remain in the disputed territories leads to the viewing of most, if not all, Palestinians as enemies, and anyone who is connected to the enemy is a fair target.

COLLECTIVE PUNISHMENT

Issues related to the practice of collective punishment (where this involves punishing innocents who are part of the collective) appear in a number of instances in Jewish sources.

One could consider our forefather Avraham as the first "conscientious objector to collective punishment" for his refusal to participate in or condone collective punishment. He was even willing to risk punishment himself in order to try to dissuade G-d from His intention to mete out collective punishment to Sodom and Gomorrah. His argument with G-d is described in Genesis:

> If there are fifty righteous within the city, will You indeed sweep away and not forgive the city for the fifty? . . . It is far from You to do such a thing, to slay the righteous with the wicked. . . . Shall not the Judge of all the earth do justly? (Genesis 18:24–25).

Here Avraham courageously questions G-d and appeals His decision to destroy entire cities. Avraham's questioning of the impending collective punishment succeeded in persuading G-d, so to speak, to reconsider. The implication is that collective punishment, where it includes innocents, is not acceptable, and only those who have sinned should be punished for their own wrongdoing.

Avraham held himself to a very high standard. He feared that he may have killed innocent people during the wars he waged (described in Genesis 14). According to midrash Tanhuma:

Avraham excoriated himself mercilessly, saying, "Perhaps among those whom I have killed there were some righteous men . . ." (Tanhuma 3:14 on Genesis 15:1)

MASSACRE IN NABLUS

This principle of not harming innocents appears elsewhere in the Torah. Our forefather Yaakov severely rebuked two of his sons, Shimon and Levi, when they massacred the city of Shechem (Shechem is Nablus today) as a form of revenge. This act of reprisal, shading over to vicious vindictiveness, was executed by the two brothers as retribution for the rape of their sister Dinah. Despite this seeming justification tendered by the brothers, Yaakov censured his sons in one of the most caustic statements in the Bible, when he reproved them:

Shimon and Levi are brothers; weapons of violence are the means of their livelihood. Let my soul not be coupled with theirs; into their assembly let my glory not be united. For in anger they slew men, and in their willfulness they continued in their destruction of cattle. Cursed be their anger, for it was fierce, and their wrath for it was cruel. (Genesis 49:5–7).

Yaakov was shaken by what his sons did, and does not mince words in his reproach. Similar words might be said in reaction to our attempts to justify aerial bombing of Palestinian cities as retribution for attacks by terrorists. If we do not want to be cursed, we have to decline to participate in these actions, even if we have to refuse to serve in the territories altogether.

The argument is made that we have no choice and that the IDF must take such steps to preserve the security of the state. I cannot be convinced that the existence of the State of Israel hangs on the killing of children in refugee camps. The rule over another nation, a hostile population, does not strengthen our defensive posture; rather it weakens us. It prolongs the necessity for curfews and blockades of millions of humans, for abrogation of their elementary rights, and for physically injuring them.

In the case of Shimon and Levi, they defended their action as being of deterrent value. Yaakov rejects this argument because even in military conflicts there are acts that are prohibited. This can be derived from the comments of Ramban (Nachmanides) on the episode. He discusses the claim, heard today as well, that Shimon and Levi were justified in attacking and murdering the men of Nablus and sacking the city because the citizens did not bring the rapist to justice. After discussing this line of defense of Shimon and Levi, Ramban rejects it unequivocally. There is no justification for harming innocents. This is a basic tenet of justice.

Contrast Shimon and Levi's headstrong cruelty with the earlier introspection of their father. Yaakov feared killing innocents. When his brother Esau approached Yaakov with 400 armed men for a face-off, we are told that "Yaakov was greatly afraid and was distressed" (Genesis 32:7). Rashi explains the seeming redundancy (afraid and distressed) by saying that Yaakov was afraid he might be killed, and distressed that he might kill Esau, in the event that Esau had innocent intentions.

INDIVIDUAL RESPONSIBILITY: A RELIGIOUS NORM

The concept of individual responsibility for wrongdoing is encapsulated in the prohibition towards the end of the Torah:

> The fathers shall not be put to death for the children, neither shall the children be put to death for the fathers; every man shall be put to death for his own sin. (Deuteronomy 24:16)

This moral and religious norm appears elsewhere in the Tanakh. For example, the prophet Ezekiel warns:

> The soul that sins, it shall die. The son shall not bear the iniquity of the father, neither shall the father bear the iniquity of the son: the righteousness of the righteous shall be upon himself, and the wickedness of the wicked shall be upon himself alone. (Ezekiel 18:20)

This pertains to all Jews (and is not restricted to "teary-eyed left-wing liberals"). In the territories we are violating this precept daily by destroying houses of families of terrorists, preventing food and medical supplies from reaching villages, and physically harming blameless civilians—acts that would be forbidden under the rubric of "the wickedness of the wicked shall be upon himself alone."

This dilemma has preoccupied military officers around the world in the past as much as it baffles us today. How can you fight an enemy that intentionally blurs the lines between the military and the civilian, an enemy that uses that very ambiguity to its own advantage? It would be simplistic to dismiss all military operations that affect civilians as morally indefensible, especially in the context of vicious guerrilla and terrorist attacks. This conundrum has always been with us. For example, a member of the pre-state Jewish Special Night Squads (which were trained to fight Arabs by British Major General Orde Wingate) observed, "The problem of punishment and . . . the morality of battle was something that concerned Wingate greatly. On the one hand, he demanded that the innocent not be harmed. On the other hand, he knew that he faced a dilemma: Can one observe this rule in battle against gangs that receive assistance from the residents of the villages?"

I wish that I could agree with those settlers who claim that we can humanely and fairly occupy and rule those over-the-Green-Line portions of the Land of Israel, as precious to me as it is to them. But there ain't no such animal as an "enlightened occupation." The rule over three million antagonistic people, stripped of their rights, will necessitate, *nolens volens,* cruelty on our part. It will require us to violate normative prohibitions of Jewish law. Therefore the refusal to participate in actions directly related to the occupation is a religious imperative. We hope that every soldier, in the standing army and in the reserve, will ponder these dilemmas and draw conclusions himself.

BLIND OBEDIENCE TO ONE'S COUNTRY

Blind compliance can lead to bestiality, for animals live without morality and law. While there is a halakhic principle that the law of the land is obeyed when it does not contradict Jewish law *(dina demalkhuta dina),* obedience to the state is not an ultimate Jewish value. The Prophets railed against those regimes in the Jewish past that used their powers to the disadvantage of weak populations. They did not hesitate to call for disobedience to such wicked regimes: See, for example, the episode over Navot's vineyard involving Ahab and Jezebel in I Kings 21. Law-abiding citizenship is encouraged; but obedience per se as a value is not sacrosanct.

Questions of immorality and illegality waft above the orders to serve in the territories. We must continue to serve in the IDF, as a defense army, but not as an occupying force committing crimes against humanity.

We dare not become soldier robots. We may have to suffer the consequences of refusal, which can run the gamut from ridicule and social ostracism to imprisonment. As soldiers we not only have to obey orders, we also have to be aware that they may violate our most basic moral, legal, and religious norms.

February 2002

Part Four

ESCALATION: DISPATCHES FROM THE WAR OF OCCUPATION

23

THE HIDDEN WEAPONS FACTORIES

Amira Hass

THERE'S ONE LABORATORY for ticking bombs that the Shin Bet and European foreign ministers skipped when they demanded that Arafat take action against terrorism. At this lab—which has hundreds of branches in the West Bank and Gaza—hundreds, if not thousands, of people are making the mistake of thinking, "I'm ready to die with the Philistines."

The labs are the IDF checkpoints and blockades, which gradually have tightened the siege around every Palestinian settlement, making Avigdor Lieberman's plans for the cantonization of the territories look like a humane and enlightened program.

It's difficult to grasp all the information that comes from these besieged places. The lack of medical supplies, such as oxygen tanks, is a daily, desperate routine in the hospitals. Cooking gas and fuel and even drinking water routinely run out. Suppliers have difficulties bringing in fresh food.

Last week, the order went out that Palestinians are banned from using roads in Area C—some sixty percent of the West Bank. Schools are half-empty. At Fowar refugee camp, for example, the children couldn't avoid the checkpoints and couldn't get to their school in Hebron for three days. The universities are partially or fully paralyzed, like Bir Zeit, where all the roads leading to the school have been closed because of the curfew on northern Ramallah. The school year has already been lost, and along with it the students' expensive tuition.

Along with the checkpoints, closures, and curfews, an unknown number of people have lost their jobs in the private sector or have been forced to move, wasting half a salary on a second rent. Every peasant farmer who goes out to work his fields risks his life, whether he has to go through Area C or because his presence on a security road for a nearby settlement turns him automatically into a "suspect."

The IDF counts every Palestinian mortar and land mine, but doesn't count all the stun grenades and tear-gas grenades, rubber-coated bullets and live ammunition used by soldiers every day to enforce a total closure.

The northern neighborhoods of Ramallah have been under curfew for the last nine days. The soldiers in their tanks enforce that order every few hours by rolling into the middle of the road and aiming their cannons toward the hundreds of people trying to get to the city center through the hills. Sometimes the soldiers throw a tear-gas grenade or a stun grenade, sometimes they shoot "rubber." Sometimes they confiscate the keys to cars and tell the drivers to pick up the keys at the Civil Administration. But the Civil Administration building is in Area C, where Palestinians are forbidden to go.

Without cameras and outside observers, it's as if these things never happened. The IDF can promise that it knows nothing about any shooting. Like the shots that killed taxi driver Marwan Lahluh from Arabe, who tried to get to besieged Jenin via dirt roads and was shot in the chest by a bullet from a grove where the Palestinians say an IDF unit is posted.

The IDF promises that "humanitarian" cases are allowed through the checkpoints. If so, how come Tamer Kuzamer, a sick baby, and his mother were not allowed through the Habla checkpoint to get to a doctor in Ramallah? His family looked for a roundabout way, much longer than the direct one, but the baby died en route. Why did two heart patients on their way back to Gaza from medical treatment end up waiting three hours last Friday night until an Israeli lawyer's intervention finally enabled them back into the besieged Strip? And why should a woman, who gave birth only fourteen hours earlier, have to wait in an ambulance for hours at the exit from Nablus on the way back to a village only ten minutes away by car? When there are no journalists or diplomats around, the IDF's answer is that "the complaints are not known to us."

Every one of these examples should be multiplied by tens of thousands of people, who are daily subjected to the same harm, in order to begin to understand the totality of the Israeli siege. One has to imagine the eyes of all those who see an old man tottering on crutches in the mud and rain as he shrinks past a huge tank, or a young girl with pigtails and in a school uniform, cowering behind a rock as a soldier throws tear gas.

Israel has but one answer: All is fair in the war against terrorism. That's why it's forgotten that the suicide terrorists near the Jerusalem hotel and on the Haifa bus slipped into Israel despite the checkpoints, and that the Jerusalem pedestrian-mall bombers came from Abu Dis, which is in full Israeli security control. And that's apparently why there will be only more military escalation and a further tightening of the closure.

December 12, 2001

24

THE CHECKPOINTS OF ARROGANCE

Meron Benvenisti

ON MARCH 3, 2002, seven soldiers and three settlers were killed by a single Palestinian sniper at Wadi Haramiyeh, an isolated northern West Bank checkpoint near the settlement of Ofra. Hours later, another soldier was killed in an Islamic Jihad attack on a Gaza Strip checkpoint. These attacks followed a February 20 raid on a checkpoint near Ramallah that left six soldiers dead.

The tragic failures exposed by the killing of Israel Defense Forces troops at checkpoints at the hands of Palestinian guerrillas released a flood of criticism, which forced the military command to learn some lessons and initiate changes in the management and tactics of the roadblocks.

Presumably, these lessons will be implemented and the defensive and security measures, together with the supervision of the checkpoints, will be enhanced. But it is impossible to expect the investigators to go so far as to recommend eliminating the checkpoints, and not because they come to the conclusion that the checkpoints have enormous military importance, nor because the settlers insist on keeping the checkpoints in place because they "provide a sense of security for people on the roads" of the West Bank.

The checkpoints will remain the main point of contact and friction between the occupying power and the rebellious population not because they serve any security purpose, but because their function is to send a message of force and authority, to inspire fear, and to symbolize the downtrodden nature and inferiority of those under the occupation.

The large blocks of cement, the fortified positions and the half-dozen or so frightened soldiers at a checkpoint are nothing but a show-case intended to display who has the power to rule the lives of those under rule, or even to cause their deaths—and almost without the use of real force, but rather by relying on the anxiety of the occupied, who have been coerced into agreeing to behave in accordance with the rules dictated by the agents of power.

The scorn for the Palestinians and the arrogant reliance on the mentality of subservience are expressed not only by virtue of the checkpoints' existence, but also their locations. The checkpoint at Wadi Haramiyeh was there because nobody ever considered the possibility that the Palestinians were capable of exploiting the tactical inferiority of its positioning, expecting them only to wait quietly in line, obsequious to the troops. How dare they break the rules, smash the display and expose the checkpoint as a pathetic symbol of control through force?

Colonial regimes have always been based on the arrogance of a few soldiers controlling the lives of millions of subjects through minimal use of force and reliance on a "deterrence" that perpetuates the inferiority of those under their rule. Such regimes can last as long as the subjects agree to behave in accordance with the dictates from above. But the moment the rules of the game are broken and the checkpoints turn from displays of control into barricades of revolt, small groups of soldiers do not have a chance of remaining anything more than props for their commanders' arrogant contempt.

After hundreds of thousands of people who line up obsequiously in long, winding lines between cement blocks rise up and refuse to show their ID cards or obey the order to turn back, and are ready to pay with their lives for their revolt, commissions of inquiry will be established to find out how such a powerful army lost the battle for the checkpoints.

The lesson learned by the British in India (and the lesson learned by all the other arrogant colonialists) won't be considered relevant because the checkpoints here are intimately connected to the settlements, and the security of the settlements and the approaches to them must be guaranteed at all cost. Thus, the mentality of those who established the checkpoints—based on a colonialist attitude toward the Palestinians—is the same mentality that established the settlements, based on the belief that an unctuous Palestinian inferiority would last forever.

Those who planted the settlements in the Katif Bloc [in Gaza] or in the heart of Samaria and northern Judea [the West Bank] assumed the Palestinians would forever remain obsequious; otherwise, how could one explain the logic of establishing Jewish islands in the heart of Arab populations?

The settlers argue that from the very beginning, Zionism flew in the face of reality. It succeeded, they say, precisely because it ignored reality and never surrendered to the rational concepts of reality that predicted failure for the cause. Therefore, the demographic and geographic arguments used against the settlers evaporated in the fervor of their vision.

But now it turns out that others can alter reality through the power of commitment to a nationalist ideology; the attempt to claim a monopoly on ideals, in the false belief that the other will not and cannot rebel, leads to irreparable disaster.

The so-called settlement enterprise, like the checkpoints set up to save it, will pass from this world because the wheel has turned: Now, the Palestinians are the ones who are rising up against reality, refusing to surrender to rational perceptions of the balance of power that predict their failure. And they have a good role model.

March 7, 2002

25

BALATA HAS FALLEN

Ze'ev Sternhell

THERE WAS SOMETHING surreal about the television appearance, last Saturday night, by the commanders of the two brigades that operated in the refugee camps of the northern West Bank. The commander of the paratroop brigade declared: Balata camp has surrendered. Indeed, the refugee camp was "conquered" by elite forces, using state-of-the-art weaponry, and backed up by tanks, armored personnel carriers and helicopters. If the whole thing were not sad and grotesque, it would be amusing.

But this is a story that is characteristic of the road that has been followed by heroic little Israel, which was admired by the whole Western world, until this terrible period. There were times when the paratroopers were known as the fighters of the Mitla Pass, Ammunition Hill and the Chinese Farm. The Golani Brigade used to be famed for breaching the fortifications of Rafah, as the fighters of Tel el Faher and the Hermon outpost. Their sons and grandsons have fallen to the level of breachers of walls in shacks built of blocks and boards. And they are no longer ashamed to speak of war when what they are really engaged in is colonial policing, which recalls the takeover by the white police of the poor neighborhoods of the blacks in South Africa during the apartheid era.

There was a time—on the first day of the 1967 Six-Day War—when the commander of a tank company in 7th Brigade, Avigdor Kahalani, stopped his tank column in the midst of the advance near Rafah so he wouldn't run over two frightened Bedouin children. He waited until their mother came to collect them. Later that day, Kahalani's tank was hit and he suffered extensive burns. To the division commander, Major General Israel Tal, the behavior of the young officer, and not just his fighting, was exemplary.

Today, again near Rafah, army men of a different generation watch as children play next to a booby-trapped bomb [on November 23, 2001] that was placed there by the IDF and don't lift a finger. It must have been clear to all of them that if the children touched the bomb it would explode, with loss of life. When the military advocate general finally decided to launch an investigation into the incident—in which five children were killed—the division commander did everything in his power to prevent the probe from taking place.

In colonial Israel, and more especially the Israel in which advocates of "transfer" sit in the government, human life is cheap—and therein lies the most serious danger to our future. A society in which dozens of children are killed as a result of army operations can easily lose its last remaining moral inhibitions. The fact that the Palestinians are also killing indiscriminately cannot absolve us of responsibility for what is going on in the territories. The killing of innocent people is gradually becoming a norm, and that norm is being implemented in the service of a goal that seeks to deprive another people of its freedom and its human rights: The Sharon government is turning the territories into one huge jailhouse, and is turning its citizens into wardens who are called upon to suppress a prisoner uprising. That was not quite the purpose of Zionism.

If the army is dominated by shamelessness, and if purely military actions by the Palestinians, such as successful attacks on army outposts and checkpoints, are included under the rubric of terrorism, the settlers' camp is doing all it can to label our inability to cope with the Palestinians' war of independence as the "Rosh Hashanah War." This half-baked attempt to create symmetry between a just war and a campaign of colonialist suppression is not merely a curiosity: It is the desecration of the memory of those who fell in the 1973 Yom Kippur War. It won't be long before we are told that the battle in which tank crews risked their lives on the banks of the Suez Canal and the effort in which an Israeli tank destroys a Palestinian car containing a mother and her three children is the same war.

We should take note here of an interesting phenomenon. The number of Israeli civilian casualties in the past year is far greater than the number of soldiers who have been killed or wounded. When all is said and done, the army is waging a deluxe war: It is bombing and shelling defenseless cities and villages, and that situation is convenient for both the army and the settlers. They are well aware that if the army were to sustain casualties on the same scale as occurred in Lebanon, we would now be on our way out of the territories.

We perceive the death of civilians in shooting attacks or at the hands of crazed suicide bombers in the heart of our cities, including the extinction of whole families, as a decree of fate or as a kind of act of nature. However, the death of soldiers immediately poses the critical question: What are the goals of the war? For what end are the soldiers being killed? Who sent them to their death? As long as the conscript troops do not pay too heavily, as long as the reservists are not called up in massive numbers to protect and defend the occupation, the question of "why" does not dictate the national agenda.

However, the atmosphere in the country is rapidly approaching the boiling point. More and more people are beginning to understand that the Israeli reprisal operations only engender despair, and despair gives rise to suicide bombers. Today, when the whole political system is paralyzed, it looks as though it will be possible to bring an end to the madness that is raging here only if people take to the streets en masse and demand an immediate start to negotiations.

March 8, 2002

26

ARE THE OCCUPIED PROTECTING THE OCCUPIER?

Amira Hass

IN RECENT DAYS, the IDF and armed groups of Palestinians have displayed a common interest in presenting a distorted picture of reality. Both sides are greatly exaggerating when they talk about "Palestinian military resistance" to the IDF incursions into the refugee camps—and yesterday into Ramallah—referring to "battles" and "firefights."

But in Qalqilyah and Deheisheh, where a conscious and level-headed decision was made not to take part in the show called "resisting and repelling the military invasion," the military could not talk about a "battle" or "combat." Nonetheless, when it was reported that two Palestinians were killed in Qalqilyah, there was an automatic slip of the tongue and it was said they "died in a firefight." But there were no such battles in the town.

That doesn't mean that in some of the camps, and now in Ramallah, armed Palestinians did not try to respond with fire to the Israeli forces. But the heavy price paid by the families of those IDF soldiers killed in the recent raids helps erase the real picture—the IDF is not conducting battles in the territories. At most, the IDF, with all its sophisticated advanced weaponry, has encountered a few groups and individuals armed with much inferior weaponry and with only the most elementary military training in combat tactics.

For the armed groups of Palestinians, it is important to present their actions as an "uprising." They confuse their desire to pick up weapons and die for what they are convinced is their war of independence, and the results of their readiness to battle one of the strongest armies in the world.

For the IDF and the Israeli government it is important to speak about fighting and to give the impression that both sides are equals, thus burying the fact that most of the Palestinian dead are civilians or members of the security forces who, even if they were armed, stayed out of the fighting. And it is especially important for the army and government to bury the fact that the IDF in the territories is an occupying power. Only thanks to its far superior strength is Israel able to continue controlling the lives of three million Palestinians, guaranteeing the existence of the settlements on the Palestinians' land.

The gap between the bragging by both sides—the IDF's and the armed Palestinians—and the limited achievements, on the Palestinian side, of their guerrilla attacks on soldiers is what pushes most Palestinians into support for the suicide bombers inside Israel and against Israelis. These lethal attacks are perceived as the only significant response to IDF actions deep inside civilian Palestinian populations. But they are also an admission of the limits of the armed resistance to the Israeli occupation.

Most Palestinians know their youths are bragging. But apparently in Israel, the belief that the IDF is indeed involved in a war—in other words, in something "symmetrical"—is based on the fact that Israelis like to regard the Palestinian Authority as a sovereign political entity.

That wrong impression has deep roots in the years of the Oslo process and a distorted view of reality that was fostered in Israel during those years. Israel very quickly got rid of its civic duties to the occupied population, which remained occupied because the IDF remained the sovereign in all the 1967 areas. It was called "transferring civilian authority." The PA was given responsibility for civic affairs, like sewage, education, and road building, for three million Palestinians. Thus, the Israeli and Western public could believe there had been an "end to the occupation."

But Israel—and the West—paid no attention to the fact that it was administrative control over people without authority over most of the area in which they lived, and without any room for development, a requirement for every government. Israelis and the West also did not notice—or know—that nearly every administrative function by the PA required approval by the Israeli authorities. Israel and the world saw the outer trappings of sovereignty—a flag, an airport, jails, security forces, and show trials—as proof that Palestinian sovereignty had been established. Forgotten was the fact that Israel controlled—and continues to control—all the external borders, the passages inside the West Bank and from it to Gaza and back, the water sources, the economy, the movement of population into the territories, and the registration of the Palestinian population.

Like the partnership between the IDF and the armed Palestinian fighters who make claims of "battles" when there are none, so has the partnership between Israeli governments and the Palestinian leadership wanted to present the PA areas as politically independent, describing Area A as "free of occupation." The second intifada was a direct result of that false portrayal of reality.

Continued Israeli control did not disturb and still does not disturb the Israeli public from regarding the "autonomous" areas of the limited, fragmented, cantonized territory, which has been splintered into enclaves cut off from one another, as a "state." A "state" with equal responsibility—indeed more—than its "neighbor," Israel, but without equal rights. A "state" that is perceived as an aggressor. Thus, we've reached the point where the occupied are being told it is up to them to guarantee the peace and security of the occupiers.

March 14, 2002

27

A QUEUE OF BOMBERS

Uri Avnery

WHEN A WHOLE people is seething with rage, it becomes a dangerous enemy, because the rage does not obey orders.

When it exists in the hearts of millions of people, it cannot be cut off by pushing a button.

When this rage overflows, it creates suicide bombers—human bombs fueled by the power of anger, against whom there is no defense. A person who has given up on life, who does not look for escape routes, is free to do whatever his disturbed mind dictates. Some of the suicide bombers are killed before they reach their goal, but when there are hundreds of them, thousands of them, no military means will restore security.

The actions of Chief of Staff Mofaz during the last month have brought this rage to an unprecedented pitch and instilled it into the hearts of every Palestinian, be he a university professor or a street boy, a housewife or a high-school girl, a leftist or a fundamentalist.

When tanks run amok in the center of a town, crushing cars and destroying walls, tearing up roads, shooting indiscriminately in all directions, causing panic to a whole population—it induces helpless rage.

When soldiers crash through a wall into the living room of a family, inducing shock among children and adults, ransacking their belongings, destroying the fruits of a life of hard work, and then break the wall to the next apartment to wreak havoc there—it induces helpless rage.

When soldiers shoot at everything that moves—out of panic, out of lawlessness, or because Sharon told them "to cause losses"—it induces helpless rage.

When officers order troops to shoot at ambulances, killing doctors and paramedics engaged in saving the lives of the wounded, bleeding to death—it induces helpless rage.

When these and thousands of other acts like them humiliate a whole people, searing their souls—it induces helpless rage. And then it appears that the rage is not helpless after all. The suicide bombers go forward to avenge, with a whole people blessing them and rejoicing at every Israeli killed, soldier or settler, a girl in a bus or a youngster in a discotheque.

The Israeli public is dumbfounded by this terrible phenomenon. It cannot understand it, because it does not know (and perhaps does not want to know) what has happened in the Palestinian towns and villages. Only feeble echoes of what is really happening have reached it. The obedient media suppress the information, or water it down so that the monster looks like a harmless pet. Television, which is now subject to Soviet-style censorship, does not tell viewers what is going on. If somebody is allowed to say a few words about it, for the sake of "balance," the words are drowned in a sea of chatter by politicians, commentators acting as unofficial spokespersons, and the generals who caused the havoc.

These generals look helplessly at a struggle they do not understand and make arrogant statements divorced from reality. Pronouncements like "We have intercepted attacks," "We have taught them a lesson," and "We have destroyed the infrastructure of terrorism" show an infantile lack of understanding of what they are doing. Far from "destroying the infrastructure of terrorism," they have built a hothouse for rearing suicide bombers.

A person whose beloved brother has been killed, whose house has been destroyed in an orgy of vandalism, who has been mortally humiliated before the eyes of his children, goes to the market, buys a rifle for 40,000 shekels (some sell their cars for this) and sets out to seek revenge. "Give me a hatred gray like a sack," wrote our poet Nathan Alterman, seething with rage against the Germans.* Hatred gray like a sack is now everywhere.

Bands of armed men now roam all the towns and villages of the West Bank and the Gaza Strip, with or without black masks (available for ten shekels in the markets). These bands do not belong to any organization. Members of Fatah, Hamas and the Jihad team up to plan attacks, not giving a damn about the established institutions.

Anyone who believes that Arafat can push a button and stop this is living in a dream world. Arafat is the adored leader, now more than ever, but when a people is seething with anger he cannot stop it either. At best, the pressure cooker can cool off slowly, if the majority of the people are persuaded that their honor has been restored and their liberation guaranteed. Then public support for the "terrorists" will diminish; they will be isolated and wither away.

That was what happened in the past. During the Oslo period there were attacks too, but they were conducted by dissidents, fanatics, and the public aversion to them limited the damage they caused.

American politicians, like Israeli officers, do not understand what they are doing. When an overbearing Vice President Cheney dictates humiliating terms for a meeting with Arafat, he pours oil on the flames. A person who lacks empathy for the suffering of the occupied people, who does not understand its condition, would be well advised to shut up. Because every such humiliation kills dozens of Israelis.

After all, the suicide bombers are standing in line.

March 23, 2002

---

* Nathan Alterman (1910–1970), born in Warsaw, was considered the poet laureate of the Jewish community in Palestine and the literary spokesman of the nationalist movement.

28

ON THE EVE OF THE WAR

Gideon Levy

ON THE EVE of the war, the Palestinians continued with their horrific routine. Their villages are locked behind iron gates and steel chains, with metal locks; the keys are in the hands of the Israel Defense Forces. On the main road, IDF soldiers stood and stopped those trying to sneak out, concentrating them in a ditch at the side of the road, ordering them to raise their clothes, and keeping them interminably in a kneeling position on the ground. On the hills, a convoy of donkeys transported doctors to their clinic, students to their school and old people to their homes. Samia Radi, an old woman who had suffered a serious stroke, was loaded into the trunk of the village taxi and transported like an animal, because ambulances are not allowed to enter.

On the eve of the war, the Palestinians lived humiliated in their prison, their roads open only to Jews, their sick and their expectant mothers doomed to suffering, their children to a long and arduous journey to school and their elderly to trudging through the mud. On the eve of the war, a moment before the slaughter in Netanya and the major invasion of their land, a few hours before Seder night, we toured the imprisoned villages between Qalqilyah and Nablus.

Iron gates recently replaced the dirt roadblocks and cement blocks that were here before. Dirt and cement blocks are uglier, but there is nothing like steel gates to illustrate the horror. Now the village has turned into a real prison; Habla and Azoun, Jit and Funduk, the villages along the road, are locked behind the new iron gates, with the keys in the hands of the jailer, the IDF.

Can you imagine a town like Azoun, with 9,000 inhabitants, whose only approach road is locked behind iron gates, with the keys located somewhere in the hands of an officer of the occupying army, nobody knows exactly where? Can you imagine life behind a closed iron gate? The ambulance that cannot enter, and the school bus that cannot leave? The supplies that have to be smuggled in on back roads, the merchandise that has to be smuggled out—and the basic, natural need to leave the village, which cannot be realized?

Is there a more accurate definition than that of IDF refusenik Yishai Rosen-Zvi, who called such measures "nurseries of terror"? Is there such a great distance between these iron gates and the gates of the concentration camps of our own history? Soon the great invasion will reach this place, too, will sow death and destruction, and the previous suffering and humiliation of the villagers will be as nothing compared to what is awaiting them.

Outside, the soldiers wait. A jeep with four reserve soldiers who did not refuse to serve their homeland and their army in any mission, their rifles at the ready, order anyone who tries to leave or to enter the village to kneel in the ditch at the side of the road. Schoolgirls holding their notebooks, an old man on a donkey, a young man who tried to smuggle a canister of oil home, a wagon driver with his wagon, all are kneeling in the ditch, looking at the ground, waiting for the orders of the soldiers.

"Raise your coat," "Take off your shirt," "Throw away the bag," "Come closer," "Go away," "Don't move," "Faster," "Slower," "Hold the horse." Submissive and humiliated, they obey every order. They have no choice.

Apparently, at exactly this moment, the suicide bomber Abdel Bassat Odeh left his home in the nearby refugee camp of Nur Shams, a few kilometers to the north, perhaps passing these locked villages and these humiliated villagers, on his way to sowing death among the elderly Seder night celebrants at the Park Hotel in Netanya, and bearing the message of the coming war.

Habla is locked behind an iron gate. A blue iron door is planted between two cement blocks and closes the only road to the village. The keys are not inside. An IDF armored personnel carrier stands on the main road, preventing any attempt to go in on foot. A soldier stands and shoots—yes, shoots—toward a convoy of "infiltrators" in the opposite wadi. They scatter in terror in all directions. They were trying to reach their district town, Qalqilyah, on the other side of the wadi; without access to it, their life is unbearable. The iron gate that closes Habla off also closes off several other villages along the way.

A sign in Hebrew for the Green Corner nursery by the side of the locked gate reminds us of a forgotten time—a time that now seems part of another world. It was no less surreal here last Shabbat: A boy whose ear had been bitten by a donkey was rushed from his village to this locked iron gate. His father kept the torn ear preserved in ice. The soldiers delayed the boy's passage. According to the testimony of an investigator from Physicians for Human Rights, Salah Haj Yihyah, the ear arrived at the Palestinian hospital before its owner. Wagons carrying fodder are the only Palestinian vehicle that can be seen on the Qalqilyah-Nablus road, a main Palestinian thoroughfare that has become a settlers' road.

There is a new iron gate in the town of Azoun as well. It's unpleasant, very unpleasant, to see a closed town. A Palestinian ambulance, a gift from the Canadian government, stops with a screech of tires next to the locked gate. But there's no reason to hurry. About two hours ago, the ambulance was called by a resident of Isla, one of the villages farther down the road from Azoun, to come for his mother, and only now has the ambulance from nearby Qalqilyah managed to reach the gate. There is of course no entry into the village, even for ambulances.

Inside the ambulance, her face gray, sits heart patient Amana Hatib. She is fifty-one years old, and has been on the road to the hospital in Nablus for hours. Her son is holding a letter from Dr. Mohammed al-Hassan that explains the severity of her situation to the soldiers at the checkpoint, who decide people's fates. Hatib will arrive at the hospital in Nablus only after they take out the other patient from Isla too. It's impossible now to take out one patient at a time. Hatib's son paces back and forth nervously. It's not hard to guess what he is thinking. The condition of his mother's heart is deteriorating, to judge by her face, which is becoming increasingly gray. Settlers' cars whiz by.

Two companies in Japan planned the water project for Azoun, of which only the sign now remains. The new entrance square to the town, with a stone monument in the center, is deserted.

A yellow taxi van approaches the blue iron gate. Two paramedics tell how, the week before, they received a call from another village on the road, and by the time the soldiers arrived to open the gate, which took over an hour, the patient died. They have their hands full. Samia Radi's sons are trying to take their paralyzed mother down from the baggage compartment of the taxi, onto which she was loaded on the way to the ambulance on the other side of the fence. Radi apparently became paralyzed as the result of a stroke; she is a heavyset woman of about sixty, sitting on an old wooden wheelchair. Their mother's weight makes their work hard; all her limbs are weak, and she threatens to fall from their hands. The woman's face is sealed. She stares into space. The stroke took away her power of speech, and perhaps also the awareness of what is happening around her.

"What a life we are living," mutters Habes Radi, the brother of the paralyzed woman. His sister has nine daughters and two sons. After the unloading and loading of the paralyzed woman has been successfully concluded, Radi's two sons now beg to travel with their mother to the hospital. The ambulance team is firm: The IDF allows only one companion, a woman. The face of the younger son, Haled, nineteen, who is not being allowed to accompany his mother to the hospital, says it all—expressing a mixture of fury and hatred. The brother, Habes: "In short, we're sick of it. This isn't life. I prefer to die rather than see this life." Radi's sister gets into the ambulance to accompany Samia to the hospital, but not before an armed policeman in a police van that happens to pass by carefully checks the passengers and the patients.

The entrance to the village of Tzara is blocked by a combination of cement blocks, the skeleton of a burned car, a puddle of whitish sewage water, a pile of ashes and hills of garbage. A swarm of mosquitoes rises and settles. Alongside all this, a Palestinian from East Jerusalem is loading new furniture made in the Sultani carpentry shop in Nablus (which will also be reoccupied at any moment). The furniture will be taken to stores in the area of the old Central Bus Station in Tel Aviv, to be sold to foreign workers from Africa—the last delivery before the war. The porters carry the Sultani furniture—breakfronts, cabinets and sofas wrapped in bluish plastic—a few hundred meters on foot, from the impassable checkpoint to the truck. Weapons can be transferred that way as well, if one so desires. "You, too, deserve to sleep like a king," says a sticker on the truck door, advertising an Israeli mattress.

A swarm of people are lined up on the path behind a row of almond trees. They are going on foot from the village of Jit on one hill to the village of Tzara on the next hill, on their way to and from the big city of Nablus. A parade of pedestrians—the parade of Palestinian suffering over the past year and a half. In the no-man's-land between one Israeli checkpoint and the next, there are students and teachers, doctors and patients, children and the elderly, the sick and the healthy. And at their head, the donkey. This is the year of the donkey in Falastin, a forgotten animal that is now enjoying great popularity. A donkey carrying books, a donkey carrying computers, and, above all, a donkey carrying involuntary horsemen, who pay five or six shekels for a ride from one checkpoint to the next. The sight is surreal.

An HP 1120 printer makes its way from the village of Biddya to a technician in Nablus, riding in taxis from checkpoint to checkpoint and on the back of Emjad's donkey between the checkpoints. Its owner, an engineer named Osama, walks alongside it, making sure it doesn't fall off the saddle, God forbid. They've been on the road for two hours, the engineer and the printer. Dr. Alam Shunar, an ear, nose, and throat specialist, is careful not to step into the many mud puddles on the way. This morning he left his hospital in Nablus, Rafidia, on his way to a clinic he conducts in Azoun for the surrounding villagers—an hour and a half each way. "It's been like this for a year and a half, and now you remembered to come?" fumes another passerby.

Another donkey driver comes along. "I take sick people, children, women, pregnant women, I take everyone," he says. "I want to make a living. I worked in Israel for thirty years, in Petah Tikvah. Now with the donkey. The price depends on the client. Sometimes free, sometimes five shekels, sometimes ten. I have another thirty to forty friends with their donkeys. We take turns. The donkey is four to six years old. When another tooth comes out he'll be eight to ten years old. Believe me, before I didn't know how to differentiate between a hen and a rooster.

"All the first seventy years of a person are suffering. After that, you enjoy yourself. How long will the donkey live? Life is in God's hands, even the donkey's life. I give him straw and barley at night, and grass during the day. Before I used to work for him, now the time has come for him to work for me. Happy holiday. When is the holiday? Believe me, once I used to know all your holidays, and I used to bring presents. Now I don't know anything."

In a hooded winter jacket that once was blue, the new wagon driver shifts from one side of the donkey to the other, full of optimistic smiles. He is the only one smiling here.

On the hill to Jit, the elderly walkers are having a hard time climbing. Occasionally one of them stops to breathe deeply and to rest. One of them is holding a small, new wooden slate, like the ones they used to buy us in our childhood. Around the roadblock of garbage and the sewage below, Israeli flags are flying, as though to cover up the shame.

Dozens of women are gathered in an apartment in Azoun that was turned into a clinic. They can't go to town, and therefore a gynecologist, Dr. Wahibi Shahshir, sneaks over here once a week, to the closure clinic. The ear, nose, and throat specialist will also arrive here soon, on foot. Dozens of men are standing around in groups outside in the streets, as in a town that is overflowing. Azoun is hermetically sealed with its new steel lock. Down on the main road beyond the iron gate, the reserve soldiers are faithfully fulfilling their mission: to check, to detain, to humiliate as much as possible. The farmers kneel in the ditch, with the schoolgirls alongside them. The wagon driver rolls up his shirt and waits until the soldier allows him to pull it down. On the eve of the war, a settler stops next to one of the soldiers, opens his electric-powered window, stretches back in his seat, and informs the soldier: There's an Arab traveling in the car behind me.

April 3, 2002

29

IN RAMALLAH WE FOUNDED PALESTINE

Ze'ev Sternhell

HAD PRIME MINISTER Ariel Sharon's Israel intended to grant the Palestinians the gift they so desired, and tried to help them create a national epic in the course of struggling for independence on the battlefield—it could not have done otherwise. In the streets of Ramallah and Qalqilyah legends are now being created upon which generations of haters of Israel will be raised. Tens of thousands of children are dreaming of the day they will bear arms. Thanks to the invasion of which he is the conductor, Ariel Sharon will be remembered as the real founder of the Palestinian state. Thus he will go down in history because of the fact that his real aim is not only rooting out terror but breaking the Palestinian national movement.

As far back as ten years ago, the General Headquarters of the Israel Defense Forces warned the government that there is no military solution to the uprising in the territories. Indeed, there are light years separating the mentality of those people and the frightening oversimplification evinced daily by the present government and chief of staff. All the primitive methods of using force and more force against a popular uprising have already been tried by occupying armies in the last century. The result has always been the same: Guerrilla fighters who enjoy the support of the population can easily drag a regular army, heavy-handed and insensitive, into actions that arouse even more hatred. It has always been the case that acts of oppression have only increased resistance.

In the end, the guerrilla wins a political victory because people who are fighting for their freedom always ultimately achieve their aim. Humiliated peoples arise from the ashes: Only a sick mind could hope that occupying the territories will bring an end to the guerrilla warfare and to terror.

On the one hand, it is reasonable to suppose that terror will only increase and become more sophisticated and devastating. On the other hand, a guerrilla war against the IDF, because of its massive deployment everywhere, will take on the dimensions of a general popular struggle and will earn international legitimization as a war of liberation.

In addition, the dimensions of the action are beginning to arouse serious suspicions not only from the moral or public relations perspective, but also with respect to their intrinsic wisdom. The GOC Central Command, as reported in the Hebrew edition of *Ha'aretz* at the beginning of the week by Amir Oren, has become commander of a front. No less than four division commanders were present at the evaluation of the situation he held before the beginning of the re-conquest of the West Bank from militias armed with rifles and youngsters who throw stones and Molotov cocktails. Four divisions was the size of the force that fought at the Suez Canal in the Yom Kippur War, whereas in June 1967, only three divisions sufficed, two of them of reservists, to conquer all of Sinai.

Yet this is not the main issue, but rather the fact that at a time when half a dozen generals go out to war and command unimaginably huge forces as compared to the enemy, three suicide bombers sow death undisturbed behind the lines in our three main cities. Anyone who is thinking not only about exterminating terror but also about wiping out the yearnings for independence of an entire people by using its military strength, will in the end make Haifa and Tel Aviv into battlefields. We gave up on security in Jerusalem long ago.

Here, some things that have been forgotten should be mentioned. If there was a single factor that twenty years ago prevented the occupation of West Beirut, a mad plan also formulated by Ariel Sharon, it was the action of Colonel Eli Geva, the commander of a tank brigade who gave up the command of his forces in order not to have to crush a civilian population. Eli Geva was an excellent officer for whom a glorious future was predicted. Geva's example had a deterrent effect on the top political echelons as well as within the army itself, the importance of which

cannot be exaggerated. It was then, apparently, that Prime Minister Menachem Begin began truly to understand the significance of the campaign his defense minister was conducting.

Geva's deed was not a political act but the result of a moral conclusion. The same is true of those who are refusing to serve in the territories today. These officers and soldiers are not fighting for a change in policy, and they will be the first to enlist to defend Israel: They simply cannot bear to see an infant die in a taxi unable to bring a woman in labor to the hospital in time, or to witness a tank crushing an ambulance. They are not afraid for their lives, because today it is more dangerous to go into a restaurant in a city than it is to command a tank company; they are simply unwilling to engage in the oppression of an occupied population.

Therefore, these people deserve moral support and practical help from those who, like the writer of these lines, are not at the moment calling for refusal to serve. They deserve support because of their clinging to basic human values even in these black hours. Were there a scrap of wisdom in this government, and were the army blessed with a bit more self-confidence, the objectors would be called up for reserve duty in the police or in the forces deployed to provide security in the streets. In this way this pitiful government could have taken credit for at least one sensible act.

April 5, 2002

30

THE PEOPLE'S WAR

Gideon Levy

FOR THE SECOND time in Israel's history, Ariel Sharon is leading the country into a war of choice—as pernicious as any war of choice—and nearly the entire public is following him more than willingly. When history judges this war, only a few will be able to say that they opposed it from the outset. In the last analysis, it will also be very difficult to blame Sharon for the consequences of the war, in the light of the sweeping support he has been given by the majority of Israelis.

With a huge leap in the percentage of citizens who "rely on him"—from forty-five percent in March to sixty-two percent in April, according to a poll reported by the mass-circulation daily *Yediot Ahronot*—it seems that no one can express the aspirations of most Israelis like the prime minister. This is not a war that was waged by Sharon, the "warmonger," this is the war of all of us. The call that was sounded at the right wing's demonstration almost a month ago—"We want war," the kind of call that is not heard in any enlightened country—has become the general sentiment.

Israel has set out on a bewildering operation whose goal no one understands and whose end no one can guess. Nearly 30,000 men were mobilized, and they reported for duty as one man, making the refusal movement, with twenty-one refuseniks currently in jail, irrelevant. "We didn't ask why, we just came," the reservists told the prime minister, expressing the "together" syndrome that characterizes Israel at such times. Tens of thousands of men leave their homes, putting their normal lives behind them, and set out to kill and be killed—and they don't even ask why? That is the behavior of the herd.

The series of horrific suicide terrorist attacks in the heart of Israeli cities, which were preceded by brainwashing, brought about the present mess. The groundless contention that former prime minister Ehud Barak offered the Palestinians "almost everything" and in return they set in motion a wave of terrorism, has become the most widely accepted axiom in Israeli public opinion. To it was added the old assumption that "something has to be done" in the light of the terrorist attacks and that "doing something" means making use of a lot more force.

The Labor Party and the Likud joined forces in order to reach the conclusion that it was necessary to reoccupy the Palestinian cities, and to strike hard against the Palestinians to teach them a lesson in the practice of peace. Even the lying statements of the prime minister that he had done everything he could to achieve a cease-fire, while ignoring the wholesale liquidations of wanted Palestinians, were widely believed.

So we have again become one nation that speaks in one voice and doesn't ask questions, such as: Who will fight terrorism after we crush all the Palestinian security units? Who are all the "armed people" Israel is arresting, and will they become Israel's security contractors after their release? What is the infrastructure of terrorism if not the occupation, the despair and the hatred? How will the shattering blow we have delivered against the entire Palestinian population help in the war against terrorism? How will it advance the peace, or at least the security of Israelis?

The nation wanted war, and it got what it wanted. Within a few days we succeeded in sowing hate in the heart of every Palestinian, and it will not soon fade. The tens of thousands of Palestinians who are imprisoned in their homes after an unbearable year and a half, who are frightened by the sounds of gunfire and the rumbling of the tanks; the bodies that continue to be brought to the hospitals without letup; the mass arrests and the general destruction—these are now generating fierce resentment against us. The world, with the exception of the United States in the meantime, is again treating us like lepers, and public opinion in the Arab states is threatening to push their leaders into an all-out war. This is the balance of blood and terror of this operation, which has not a thing to be said to its credit, other than that it satisfies the feelings of a public that is terrified by the terrorist attacks.

The Labor Party is a full partner to everything that is happening, despite its leaders' talk about a political horizon, the Saudi plan, and the day after. The problem is not the "day after" when the acts that are being perpetrated in Labor's name today are horrendous. Meretz, Hadash, and the extra-parliamentary movements have begun to come out of their slumber lately, but have not been able to obtain mass support. Over the weekend the Peace Now organization announced that it would hold a "demonstration of tens of thousands"—but only a month from now.

Most of the press is in one of its lowest periods, not only in its near total mobilization in the cause, but also because it is not supplying the public with concrete information about what is going on an hour away. Rare shots of the suffering that the Palestinians are enduring were broadcast on Channel 2 and led the defense minister to temporarily close the territories to the Israeli media, according to a report last week.

In any event, much more about what is really going on can be gleaned from the foreign networks. The suffering of hundreds of thousands of Palestinians is hardly given expression, and the critical damage being done to the health and supply systems is barely mentioned. Again, the majority of Israelis don't have the slightest idea of what their neighbors are going through.

This is a dark time in Israel. The damage we are causing ourselves will in part be irreversible. In the not so distant future, when it becomes clear that this war was pointless, the meaningful voices of opposition will begin to be heard. But they will be too few and too late.

April 7, 2002

31

LETTER FROM ARAFAT'S COMPOUND

Neta Golan and Ian Urbina

IT IS NOT Israeli actions that have surprised the international peace observers currently holed up within Arafat's presidential compound. It is the inaction of the international community that most shocks us. Inside the pockmarked building surrounded by Israeli tanks and snipers, there is one question on everyone's mind: How many international laws does Israel need to break before the UN demands a full and immediate withdrawal?

The list of violations is reaching unprecedented levels, even for a conflict with a long history of ugly behavior on both sides. International law absolutely forbids the building of the settlements, but thirty-four new settlements have been constructed in the past year alone. Collective punishment is illegal, but Israel has now escalated from interrupting food shipments to completely shutting off water to the Palestinian city of Ramallah, endangering the lives of 120,000 people. The shelling of innocuous Palestinian civilian structures such as power plants, schools, and sewage facilities is occurring at an alarming rate. Unarmed civilians are being killed practically on a daily basis.

There are also growing reports of Israeli troops raiding hospitals and firing on ambulances and journalists. These are grave breaches of international convention. The recent experience of American newspaper correspondent Anthony Shadid is hardly uncommon. First, he was shot while in a zone under full Israeli control. The area was quiet and there was no crossfire in which to be caught. Shadid was wearing the required signs on his back and front indicating that he was with the official press as he walked away from an interview in our building. Soon after Shadid arrived at the hospital, Israeli troops raided it with machine guns drawn. He was subsequently transferred for further medical treatment, and his ambulance came under fire by Israeli soldiers manning a checkpoint.

Israel is making a mockery of the Fourth Geneva Convention, the founding legal document of international human rights law, and by its tacit acceptance, the UN is severely eroding its credibility in the region and beyond.

Those of us inside the presidential compound need help desperately. But not half as much as those on the outside who are facing the full brunt of the mass roundups and house-to-house raids. The situation cannot deteriorate much further. Medical supplies have run out. Food is scarce.

Pressure from abroad is essential, even when only on a person-by-person basis. Boycotts and letter writing work. The presence of international "human shields" throughout the occupied territories has been very important in limiting the indiscriminate nature of Israeli military actions. But nothing short of a UN demand for a full withdrawal to the 1967 UN-recognized borders will succeed in restoring calm and opening the way for peace negotiations. Only then can there be discussion of the status of Jerusalem and the Palestinian refugees. Simply pulling the troops out of the recently invaded regions will not suffice.

It is not just the Palestinians and foreigners within the compound who have been calling for a full withdrawal. Even sectors within the Israeli military have put forward this option as the only chance for peace and security for the Israeli people. In a formal "Letter of Refusal" to Sharon, several hundred Israeli soldiers, most with combat experience, advocated a full withdrawal and have stated their unwillingness to serve in the West Bank or Gaza Strip.

But Sharon does not want to listen. And in the meantime we in the compound are left, not without fear, wondering whether the international community will allow the permanent expansion of the already illegal occupation and the exile if not assassination of the Palestinian leader.

April 8, 2002

32

AFTER THE OUTRAGE AND TEARS

Gila Svirsky

FRIENDS, I JUST returned to Israel from two weeks abroad, and took two more days to get a perspective on what I see and hear, which I would now like to share with you. First, the overwhelming picture before us is of death and destruction wrought by the Israeli army in the Palestinian cities, Jenin above all. In addition to the hundreds killed and thousands wounded, we have irrefutable evidence that the Israeli army has barred ambulances from evacuating the dead and wounded, has bulldozed homes in large numbers (sometimes with the families still inside), and has withheld access to water, electricity, and phone communication for periods of a week and more. Can you imagine life with no water, while men, women, and children are bleeding to death around you? And finally having to bury the corpses in an empty lot nearby, after days of keeping them at home? These go well beyond the ongoing acts of brutality, mass arrests, vandalism, theft, and humiliations, which are also rampant. A senior officer was quoted in *Ha'aretz* today as saying, "When the world sees pictures of what we have done there, it will cause enormous damage to us." It's no wonder that the media are not given access.

Listening to the report from the field at the emergency board meeting of B'Tselem last night, I was not the only one with tears in my eyes. This is no time for analysis, although I have much to say: about the complicity of Peres, about the appalling anti-Semitism unleashed internationally by legitimate anger at Israel, and about how horrifying terrorism in Israel and the so-called "war against terrorism" in the United States have given license to what is happening. Introduce Bush-Cheney-Rice-Sharon-Mofaz, and the recipe for *violence begets more violence* is complete. Today's killing of thirteen Israeli soldiers in Jenin only drives home the tragic futility of Israel's military might. Rather than analyze, this is a time to act. Here in Israel, the peace and human rights movement is working tirelessly on every imaginable front. Soldiers who refuse to serve the occupation are going to jail; convoys of food and medical supplies hastily collected have been distributed and more are being collected; human rights workers are risking their lives to monitor action; peace activists have braved hailstorms of tear gas and stun grenades in facing army checkpoints; foreign activists have served as human shields throughout the territories.

In my history of activism, I recall no parallel sense of urgency, in which lives and daily bread are being set aside to pursue a cause. But I also recall no parallel feeling that a calamity of our own making is unfolding before our eyes. I implore you to take action of your own.

Finally, I can't help but note that Israel marked Holocaust Memorial Day today. When will we finally extricate ourselves from this trauma and apply ourselves to instilling its true lesson, that of tolerance?

April 9, 2002

33

WHAT KIND OF WAR IS THIS?

Amira Hass

IT IS STILL impossible to know how many people are buried under the ruins in the Jenin refugee camp, where the smell of decomposing bodies mingles with the stench of garbage and the scent of geraniums and mint.

Leaning on a cane, a man stood on a huge pile of ruins: a jumble of crushed concrete, twisted iron rods, shreds of mattresses, electric cables, fragments of ceramic tiles, bits of water pipes, and an orphaned light switch. "This is my home," he said, "and my son is inside." His name is Abu Rashid; his son is Jamal, thirty-five and confined to a wheelchair. The bulldozer began to gnaw into the house when members of the family were inside it. And where would they be, if not in the house, seeking—like all the inhabitants of the refugee camp in Jenin— the safest place to hide from the firing of the mortars and the rockets and the machine guns, waiting for a brief respite?

Abu Rashid and the other members of his family hurried to the front door, went out with their hands up and tried to yell to the huge bulldozer, the operator of which was unseen and unheard, that there were people inside. But the bulldozer did not stop roaring, retreating a bit and then attacking again, returning and taking a bite out of the concrete wall, until it collapsed on Jamal before anyone could save him.

All around Abu Rashid other people were climbing up or down heaps of rubbish, making their way between piles of cement, sharp iron wires and fragments of metal, concrete pillars and ceilings that had collapsed, fragments of sinks. Not all of them were as introverted as Abu Rashid, who talked to himself more than he talked to those who stopped to listen to him. There were those who tried to rescue something from the ruins: a garment, a shoe, a sack of rice. Nearby, a young girl almost stumbled on a pile of broken cement blocks, pointed at the ceiling, at her feet, and wept and wept. Between the wails, she managed to say that this had been her parents' home and that she does not know who is buried under it, who had managed to get away, whether anyone was alive under the ruins, who would get them out, or when.

Among the piles of ruins, and in the midst of some houses that were still partially standing, the walls that had not collapsed riddled with numerous bullet holes of all sizes, a broad expanse had been created. Where, up until two weeks ago, several houses had stood, some of them three stories high, one or more Israel Defense Forces bulldozers had gone over the piles of cement several times, flattened them, ground them to dust, "made a 'Trans-Israel Highway,' " as A.S. put it. His home had also fallen victim to the bulldozers' teeth. Someone indicates a small opening in one pile of rubble. From it he had heard cries for help until Sunday night. On Monday morning there were no longer any sounds coming from it. Someone else points to what had formerly been a house where two sisters lived. Someone says that they are crippled. It is still unknown whether they are under the ruins or whether they got out of the camp in time.

There are houses that were empty of inhabitants when they were demolished. In some cases the soldiers ordered people to leave immediately, so they would not get killed. One old man, people say, refused to leave his home. "Fifty years ago you expelled me from Haifa. Now I have nowhere to go," they report he had said. The soldiers lifted the stubborn old man bodily and hauled him out. And there were cases in which they did not bother to issue a warning—and the bulldozers came. Without announcing over the bullhorns, without checking whether anyone was inside. This happened on Sunday, April 14, to the members of the Abu Bakr family, who live on the thin line between the refugee camp and the city of Jenin proper.

In both city and camp, a curfew had been imposed; soldiers were circulating in tanks and armored vehicles and on foot, shooting from time to time, tossing stun grenades or blowing up suspicious objects. But relative to the previous week it was quiet: There was no longer any firing from helicopters, no more exchanges of fire with a handful of armed Palestinian activists. But all of a sudden, at four o'clock in the afternoon, the members of the Abu Bakr family heard the sound of a wall being crushed. The father of the family went outside, waved a white flag and yelled to the soldiers: "We are in the house; where do you want us to go, why are you demolishing our home with us inside?" They yelled at him: "Yallah, yallah, get inside," and stopped the bulldozer.

This narrow seam where the house is located, several meters wide, has in recent days served as a transit bridge from the city to the refugee camp. The residents of the city, many of whom come from the refugee camp, tried to evade the soldiers and bring their relatives and friends water, food, and cigarettes. At the Abu Bakrs' home they concluded that the soldiers wanted to expand the area that separates the city from the camp in order to prevent "smuggling" of one sort or another. In the evening, an armored vehicle was positioned next to the house and soldiers combed the surrounding courtyard. Then the armored vehicle left. M. went to make coffee. He managed to put a teaspoon of sugar into the narrow-necked, long-handled coffeepot and began to stir the boiling water when someone or something came quickly in through the window, broke the glass and set the kitchen on fire. A stun grenade? A tear-gas grenade? Did the soldiers outside think someone was firing at them when he lit the gas burner? M. thanks God that only his hands and face were burned in the flames that were immediately extinguished, and that other people in the family weren't hurt, and that the house was not destroyed.

Mohammed al-Sba'a, seventy, was not so lucky. On Monday, April 8, the bulldozers thundered near his home in the Hawashan neighborhood, in the middle of the camp. He went out of his house to tell the soldiers that there were people inside—he and his wife, his two sons, their wives and seven children. He was shot in his doorway, hit in the head and killed, related one of his sons this week. Members of his family managed to bring him inside. But then they were ordered to come out:

The men were arrested, and then released and taken to the village of Ru-mani, northwest of Jenin. The women were taken to the Red Crescent building. The father's body remained in the house. When the men of the family returned from arrest, they could not find the house.

The destruction of dozens of houses by bulldozers began on Satur-day, April 6, four days after the Israel Defense Forces attack on Jenin began. It is not yet possible to know how many people were buried under the ruined houses. The horrible smell of dead bodies—of which new ones are being discovered every day—mingles with the stink of the garbage that has not been collected, the garbage that has been burnt and the surprising smells of geraniums, roses and the mint that grows near the bougainvillea that people cultivated in the narrow strips of ground between the crowded houses. When the time comes, the UN Relief and Works Agency and the Red Cross will make lists of the de-tained, the wounded, and the missing. But the most urgent mission right now is the distribution of water, food, and medicines. The camp has been defined as a disaster area.

The demolition of the homes by bulldozers was preceded by heavy shooting and shelling from tanks, from the beginning of the IDF action on the night of Tuesday, April 2. The tanks surrounded the camp, took up positions on the hill to the west of it, rumbled into the main street. Two days later, firing from helicopters began, people relate: rocket fire and submachine-gun fire. People took shelter under staircases, on the ground floor, in interior bathrooms, in storehouses near the inner courtyards. People crowded into small rooms, feeling each other in the dark, frightened. They blocked their ears and shut their eyes, cuddled the small, crying children.

When the shooting died down, they related, they went out and found their houses scorched, flames and smoke rising from them, rid-dled with holes, their floors shaky, doors and windows ripped out, win-dowpanes smashed to bits, huge holes in the front walls. The turn of the damage statistics will also come, and when it does, UN teams will tell of how many houses were destroyed by the bulldozers, how many were damaged by the shooting and whether they can be repaired or whether it is safer to demolish them altogether. How many families were in them. How many individuals.

Umm Yasser rescued a one-year-old baby from the neighbors' house, which was shelled. The baby's father, Rizk, she related, crawled out with his two legs injured and his back burned by fire. He came out with his arm stretched forward, bleeding, she said. The house was surrounded by soldiers. A military doctor or paramedic came, cleaned the wounds, bandaged them, and soldiers took him to the area of the cemetery and left him there. Neighbors who saw him gathered him up and called a doctor. They managed to get him to a hospital a week after he was wounded.

H. and her family were in their house when it was bombarded. They ran to take shelter in her father's home nearby. H. thinks that this was on April 8. People find it hard to remember exact dates; all the days of the attack have become a jumble of fear and blood and destruction, without nights or days. Y., her husband, was wounded by the shooting when he went out the door. She dragged him to her father's house. There they bandaged his leg, prayed that everything would be all right and managed to get him to a private hospital only on Sunday, April 14, evading the soldiers who patrolled the alley on foot.

A.S. was wounded in the course of performing an IDF mission: A foot patrol took him out of his house to accompany soldiers, walk ahead of them and open the doors of the neighborhood for them. A.S. did as he was told, and as he stood by one of the doors, another unit of soldiers appeared. Perhaps they thought he belonged to the *mukawamin* (insurgents, armed activists), because no one else dared to roam the streets during those first days of the IDF takeover of the camp. He was shot and wounded. For four days he lay in the home of neighbors, until his brothers managed to take him to medical care. Their home, on the second floor of the family's house on the hillside, was damaged by three to five rockets and numerous bullets. Soldiers took up positions in a tall house nearby, and shot.

His mother tells the story at length, leading visitors from one destroyed room to the next. And then she takes us out to the garden: He loved to plant things, he loved life, not death, she said of her son. Her

other sons offered the visitors fruit from the garden: pleasantly tart lo-
quats, refreshingly juicy plums. Most of the water tanks in the camp had
been hit during the first days of the shooting. The water pipes were
burst by the IDF bulldozers and the tanks. The fresh water supply was
cut off immediately. Therefore, when every drop of water must be
saved, biting into these fruits is a luxury.

Abu Riyad, fifty-one, was also enlisted, like many others, for IDF
missions. For five days he accompanied soldiers: During the day he
walked ahead of them, from door to door, knocked on the doors as the
soldiers concealed themselves behind him, their rifles aimed at the door
and at him. At night he was with them in a house they had taken over.
They handcuffed him and two soldiers guarded him, he said. At the
end of his mission, they told him to stay in a certain house, alone. All
around, the bulldozers and the tanks thundered. One of the tanks rolled
onto the house. Abu Riyad jumped to another house, leaping from one
destroyed house to another until he got to his home, which he also
found partially in ruins, from hits by three rockets. There were thirteen
people in the house when the rocket landed on it.

S. declared that she had been lucky. Her family's house was only occupied for a week, like a dozen other houses in the camp that climbs up
the hillside and the cliffs. S. is a widow who lives with her brother and
his family in a house at the western edge of the camp: four adults, ten
children. Most of the residents had left the neighborhood before the
IDF invasion. On the first and second nights soldiers took over two or
three houses adjacent to the home of S.'s family. The members of the
family took shelter in the kitchen, which they thought was the most
protected room. Suddenly, in the middle of the night, someone came in
through the wall, made a gaping hole near the floor and came in right
over the head of eight-year-old Rabiya. Windowpanes shattered and
the room was covered in dust. The fourteen people in the kitchen began
to scream. Through the hole in the wall they heard someone shouting
in Arabic: Anyone who leaves the house will die. They peeked and saw a
group of soldiers in the narrow alley. They tried to negotiate with the
soldiers; perhaps they would go out to the neighbors' house, to a safer

room, but the only answer they heard was: "Whoever leaves the house will die."

After a short while, the soldiers made a hole in the wall that leads to the staircase and came in through it. The members of the family, huddled together in one corner, looked on in astonishment as more and more soldiers came in, their faces painted black. The members of the family were put in another room, full of broken glass and dust. They were held there from the evening until early Friday morning. The soldiers, related S., did not allow them to leave the dimly lit room. When they pleaded to go to the bathroom, the soldiers brought them a pot from the kitchen. S.'s brother-in-law was arrested, and three women and their children were left alone in a house filled with strange soldiers.

At dawn, S. opened the door and discovered that the soldiers had been replaced. With hand gestures and body language she signaled that she wanted to go to the bathroom, to take the children to the bathroom, to bring food. Someone who looked to her like an officer said to go ahead. She had to make her way through any number of soldiers who were lying on the floor of her home, tiptoeing among them. The filth she found in the bathroom disgusted her. The officer who was next to her hung his head and she concluded that he was ashamed of what he saw. He went to a nearby house, where no one was home, and brought water. And he cleaned the bathroom. When they leave in about a week the soldiers will leave behind a large pile of leftovers from their rations.

During that night, when the family was locked into one room, the soldiers made a search of the house. They emptied drawers and cupboards, overturned furniture, broke the television, cut the phone line, took away the telephone and broke another hole in a wall that leads to another apartment. Along the broken wall is a picture done in watercolors that was painted by her brother-in-law's brother when he was fifteen. He drew a Swiss landscape: a lake, snowcapped mountains, evergreen trees, a deer, a house with a red-tiled roof and smoke curling from the chimney. By the shore of the lake he painted two mustached men dressed as Palestinians, riding a donkey. The date: May 10, 1995. The signature: Ashraf Abu al-Haija.

Al-Haija was killed on one of the first days of the IDF attack, hit by a rocket. On Tuesday of last week his scorched body was still lying in one of the rooms of the half-destroyed house. Al-Haija was an activist in Hamas, who together with members of other armed groups had sworn to defend the camp to the death. J. Z., two of whose nephews were among the armed men who were killed, estimates that they numbered no more than seventy. "But everyone who helped them saw himself as active in the resistance: those who signaled from afar that soldiers were approaching, those who hid them, those who made tea for them." According to him, no door in the camp was closed to them when they fled from the soldiers who were looking for them; the people of the camp, he said, decided not to abandon him, not to leave the fighters to their own devices. This was the decision of the majority, taken individually by each person.

Despite his family and emotional relationship with many of the armed men, he admits that it is hard for him to describe exactly how the fighting went in which they were killed and in which Israeli soldiers were killed. "From reconstructions that we made together, it appears to us that the army attacked the camp with tank and machine-gun fire from several directions and tried to get infantry forces in. But because of the resistance by our fighters, this failed. Then they started to attack all the houses in the camp with helicopters and tanks, indiscriminately. The soldiers that took over the houses at the edge of the camp signaled where to fire and hit." Gradually, the armed Palestinians were routed deeper into the camp, to their last battles.

J. Z. is a construction worker who built his own home and the homes of friends. His house was destroyed by direct hits from several rockets. He is sleeping at the home of his young friend, A. M. When darkness envelops the camp, whose electricity has been cut off since April 3, candlelight shines through only a few of the windows. There is an illusion that a window through which light does not shine will not be hit by shooting. IDF fire continues at intervals, though there are no longer any Palestinians who will shoot in the direction of the soldiers. From time to time the silence is shattered by the sound of an explosion. Anxiety and uncertainty are overcome in a conversation typical of these days, with A. M.'s mother and his aunt. On Monday evening the conversation with the guest from Israel began with the enumeration of those J. Z. knows were killed: Seven of them were armed men killed in battle. There were ten civilians, among them three women and at least two old men. There are scores of people whose fate is still unknown.

The conversation jumps from memories of the prison installation at Ketsiot, where J. was imprisoned during the first intifada and which has now been reopened, for soldiers. One soldier, someone had told A. M., had left his skullcap in a house he had searched. Heavy shooting enveloped the neighborhood and the house where he had forgotten the skullcap. The soldier told a young Palestinian who had been "recruited" that if he brought him the skullcap he would be released. Dodging the bullets, the young man ran to the house, brought the skullcap and was allowed to go home. J. tells another story that is going around the camp, about soldiers who were attacked from inside a house they had taken over earlier, from which they fled, leaving their weapons behind. It is said in the camp that one of them cried: "Mother, mother, what kind of war is this?"

April 18, 2002

Part Five

RESOLUTION?

34

HAIL, CAESAR!

David Grossman

CARRY ON, CAESAR. Death awaits us at every corner, but you, sir—carry on. Don't let us, with our petty lives and deaths, stand in your way. You have a plan. We're sure of it. For that reason, we feel certain that everything we see going on around us is merely a preliminary for something a lot more successful, some brilliant idea that will change the whole picture in one fell swoop.

We only look hopeless, you know. We don't really feel like the walking dead. We believe in your promise of peace, O Caesar. We feel it coming in great, winged strides. You will force our enemies to love us, no matter what we do to them. You will get rid of their leader and install someone else in his place, someone submissive and obedient. And then, in a wink, the hearts of our enemies will fill with love for us. They will forgive us for all our misdeeds, and even justify them and realize that they had a purpose.

Only please, could you hurry up a little? We aren't complaining, God forbid. We don't doubt your ability to reinvent human nature, and we know that you are the man who can mold the enemy, getting them to accept whatever we offer them, even your blank refusal to give them anything at all. Just because no people, no matter how strong, has ever managed to keep up this kind of occupation under such conditions doesn't mean it's a law of nature: We can be the first! Why not? Only we beg of you, get a move on, because soon, how should we put it, you won't have any people left. Soldiers or civilians.

Things are little rough, sir, if you've noticed, which we're sure you have. But you are strong, stronger than we are, no question. We are weak-willed and timid; what can we do? For that we need you, to lead us with your power and your army—one of the mightiest armies in the world—toward a new future, the "era of retaliatory strikes," you might call it (as we did in the 1950s). It will be a future in which every time the fedayeen strike, we will strike back! They'll hit us here, and we'll hit them there. They'll blow themselves up in our streets, and we'll send bombers out to theirs. What a brainstorm! Now that's what you call using our power to the hilt!

True, a speck of doubt creeps in sometimes, an idle thought, about the different definitions of courage and cowardice, faith and defeatism. Sometimes a small, unpatriotic devil whispers in our ear that maybe the worst kind of defeatism is our slow, almost hypnotic descent into oblivion and apathy, without even trying to pull ourselves out. Sometimes, a wagging tongue has the nerve to insinuate that even with the terrible cards in our hand right now—the despair, the barbarity of Palestinian terrorism, the settlements, that impossible Arafat—we could, somehow, play a better game. By making better use of opportunities to thaw the ice and reach a compromise. By trying to be smart, not just right. By doing something to change the situation dramatically, with the help of a bold, magnanimous, far-sighted political maneuver.

But, of course, we have an irrefutable argument for that: We've already tried! We offered them everything and all they did was spurn and betray us! Never again. We will not repeat that fatal mistake. We will always face forward, embracing the tactics and strategies that have been so successful, and brought us to where we are today.

And so, O Caesar, continue to fight until our last drop of blood. The main thing, of course, is to make the enemy bleed, too. In unison, we declare: "Let us die with the Philistines." Serves them right.

Sometimes, one has to admit, we get a little confused. Forgive us. When we hear some of your ministers demanding that the army strike back with even greater force, that we reoccupy the territories, that we send four million Palestinians into exile, we start to wonder whether your plan is so clever and sophisticated that it even has answers for the apocalypse that will take place if these ideas are implemented. We start to wonder whether, for the sake of your goals, you have made a strategic decision to move the battlefield not into enemy territory, as is normally done, but into a completely different dimension of reality—into the realm of utter absurdity, into the realm of utter self-obliteration, in which we will get nothing and neither will they. A big fat zero.

But these are only trifling thoughts. Your loyal citizens have no doubts about your wisdom and your vision. Very soon, it will become evident to all and sundry that there was a profound reason for having to live in this senseless way for years, and for agreeing to "suspend our disbelief," like in the theater, until the plot is resolved and the secret comes out. For this same unknown reason, we have permitted the undermining of our democracy, our economy, our security, and the possibility of ever having a tolerable future here.

One way or another, when we finally discover what those motives and reasons are, which are currently beyond us, we will understand why we have had to spend decades living in a world parallel to the one we were meant to live in, and why we agreed to live our one and only life in a kind of latent death. Until then, we will continue to support you with all our heart. We, who are about to die—in the dozens, the hundreds and the thousands—salute thee. Hail, Caesar!

February 22, 2002

35

INTERVIEW WITH AMI AYALON

Sylvain Cypel

AMI AYALON was the head of Israel's General Security Service (Shin Bet, or Shabak) from 1996 to 2000. This interview was conducted by Sylvain Cypel of Le Monde *in December of 2001.*

SYLVAIN CYPEL: How do you see the state of political debate in Israel?

AMI AYALON: Israeli society, top to bottom, is sinking into confusion. There are no reference points. People mask this reality with swaggering slogans: "We will vanquish terrorism!" At a colloquium, the army chief of staff declares: "We are winning"; he evokes the "superiority of Tsahal"—the Israeli army—and his "feeling that the nation is finding its strength." Then he adds, "There are today more Palestinian terrorists than a year ago," and says there will be even more tomorrow! If we are winning, how come terrorists are multiplying?

In Israel, no one is in touch with reality. This is a consequence of a misperception of the peace process. "We have been generous and they refused!" is ridiculous, and everything that follows from this misperception is skewed. Moreover, our obsession with the Palestinians makes us forget to ask questions about ourselves. What do we want to be? Where are we going? No leader addresses these questions. Thus the confusion and general anxiety.

SC: The majority of leaders, though, are convinced that time works in favor of Israel.

AA: Since September 11, our leaders have been euphoric. With no more international pressures on Israel, they think, the way is open. This obscures the consequences of our holding on to the Palestinian territories. This is not only a moral matter. Our founders saw a state that provided a homeland for Jews and was a democracy. From both points of view, time plays against us! Demographically, it works in favor of the Palestinians. And politically in favor of Hamas and the settlers. But to fight against Hamas, we must evacuate the settlers, whose proximity to the Palestinians reinforces hatred. Among the Palestinians, the weight of the Islamists is increasing, and also that of intellectuals who used to favor a two-state solution, but who now say: "Since the Israelis will never evacuate the settlements, well, then, there will be a binational state." This is something I absolutely oppose. It would not be a Jewish state anymore. And if it remained a Jewish state while dominating the Arab population, it would not be a democracy.

SC: Do you exclude the possibility of an Israeli victory, despite the power differential?

AA: We have had our "victory." In 1967, we occupied all the Palestinian lands. Once "terrorism is vanquished," what shall we do? This is absurd. The Palestinians want self-rule. Whoever wants to "vanquish" them, then offer them bread and circuses, understands nothing. The Israeli army is stronger than ever, our secret services are excellent; then why is the problem not resolved? Reoccupying the Palestinian Authority lands and killing Arafat, what would that change? Those who want victory want an unending war.

SC: Yet, since September 11, many think that Israel can change the regional situation in its favor.

AA: An illusion! September 11 has changed many paradigms in the United States, but nothing basic in the Middle East. Whatever Arafat's errors, the Palestinian people will continue to exist. As long as the Palestinian question is not resolved, the region will not know stability. Only a Palestinian state will preserve the Jewish and democratic character of Israel. We do need international political and financial help to resolve that problem and that of the refugees, because as long as the refugee problem persists, even if a Palestinian state exists, it will poison our relationship.

SC: But the Israelis are traumatized by the Palestinian demand for the return of refugees.

AA: Let us stop worrying about what our adversaries say and ask what we, ourselves, want. We do not want the return of the refugees. But we can refuse only if Israel acknowledges unambiguously its role in the suffering of the Palestinians and its obligation to help solve the problem. Israel must accept the principle of the right of return and the PLO must commit itself to not question the Jewish identity of our state.

SC: What do you think of the view put forth by the head of Mossad that Israel is in the front line of the "third world war" against terrorism?

AA: Anyone who equals Arafat with bin Laden understands neither Arafat nor bin Laden. The latter is the guru of a very harmful sect, but one that is very marginal to Islam; it aims to bring chaos and cares nothing about the international community. But Arafat dreams of being accepted by the international community—since 1993, he has constantly made reference to it, demanding the application of the UN resolutions, while we, Israelis, refuse! If bin Laden is killed, his sect may disappear with him. If we kill Arafat, the Palestinian people will continue to want their independence.

SC: Do you fear that the Palestinian territories may become a quagmire?

AA: We say the Palestinians behave like "madmen"; it is not madness but a bottomless despair. As long as there was a peace process—the prospect of an end to the occupation—Arafat could maneuver, incite or repress violence to better negotiate. When there is no more peace process, the more terrorists one kills the more strength their camp gains. Yasser Arafat neither prepared nor triggered the intifada. The explosion was spontaneous, against Israel, as all hope for the end of occupation disappeared, and against the Palestinian Authority, its corruption, its impotence. Arafat could not repress it. The peace process is what allowed Arafat to be seen as the head of a national liberation movement rather than a collaborator of Israel. Without it, he can fight neither against the Islamists nor against his own base. The Palestinians would end up hanging him in the public square.

SC: From Oslo to Camp David, did Israel miss a rare opportunity for peace?

AA: Yes. It is not all the Israelis' fault. The Palestinians, the international community, bear some responsibility, but we missed an extraordinary opportunity: The international situation was incredibly favorable after the fall of Communism, the Gulf War, the emergence of globalization. All these phenomena led Israel to reexamine its own assumptions. Now, we are regressing.

SC: Do you favor a "unilateral separation" from the Palestinians?

AA: I do not like the word "separation," it reminds me of South Africa. I favor unconditional withdrawal from the territories—preferably in the context of an agreement, but not necessarily: What needs to be done, urgently, is to withdraw from the territories. And a true withdrawal, which gives the Palestinians territorial continuity in a Transjordan linked to Gaza, open to Egypt and Jordan. If they proclaim their own state, Israel should be the first to recognize it and to propose state-to-state negotiations, without conditions, on the basis of the Clinton proposals [of December 2000], to resolve all pending problems.

December 22, 2001

36

A BLACK FLAG HANGS OVER
THE IDEA OF TRANSFER

Tom Segev

AN EVIL SPIRIT is infiltrating public discourse: the spirit of expulsion. The zealots among the settlers still mostly use the slogan "Kahane Was Right," but the slogan "No Arabs–No Terror" is representative of increasing numbers of spokesmen. It happens whenever there's a proliferation of terror attacks. Kahane relied on God, Rehavam Ze'evi on David Ben-Gurion.* Ze'evi tried to dress up his expulsion plans in the costume of decency: His planned expulsions would be "by agreement," meaning on the basis of an agreement between the State of Israel and the state that would absorb the expelled.

This week, Ze'evi's heir, former minister Benny Elon, gave up the "agreement" element: He proposed to exploit the current war and, under cover of the battles, to "evacuate" the refugee camps in the West Bank. Elon was allowed to express those views on Israel Radio.

Minister Ephraim Sneh [of the Labor Party] recently came out with a plan to transfer some Israeli Arab towns, including Umm al-Fahm, to Palestinian sovereignty. Like physical transfer, the legal transfer proposed by Sneh is an expression of the desire to get rid of all the Arabs:

---

* Rehavam Ze'evi, a veteran of 1948 and subsequent wars, founded the Moledet party, which advocates expulsion of the Palestinians, in 1988. Ze'evi was assassinated on October 17, 2001, by the Popular Front for the Liberation of Palestine in retaliation for the murder of its general secretary, Abu Ali Mustafa, in August.

those in the territories and those in Israel. While still in uniform, Dr. Sneh liked to nurture his image as one of those officers who knew how to help the Arabs. In government cabinet sessions he sounds like a Lieberman-Landau clone.

Some participants find it difficult to believe their ears. Passionately supporting that transfer concept, the minister was allowed to propose on one of the television talk shows that Israel expel relatives of suicide bombers.

Israeli law and international law do not allow a person's citizenship to be revoked. But the law is only a law, so Eli Yishai, the interior minister, is hurrying to prepare legislation that would allow the state to strip citizenship from those it chooses. One of the suicide bombers lived in the territories, but was an Israeli citizen by virtue of his parents' marriage. Yishai has already ruled that there will be no more family reunifications. He also wants to take action against residents of the territories who hold Israeli identity cards. The result could be the same as in Jerusalem: a flood of people with Israeli ID cards in the West Bank swarming into Israel, but that problem could be solved if Sneh's proposal is accepted.

This is not merely a matter of clean language. If the wave of terror propels Israel back to the troubles of the 1930s, the next stage of deterioration is possible. Leaders of the Zionist movement discussed the transfer idea; up to the War of Independence it was only written and spoken about, but there is a link between the idea and the Palestinian tragedy of 1948. In advance of the Sinai operation of 1956, plans were drawn up for the mass expulsion of Israeli Arabs from the "Triangle" [a heavily Arab region of central Israel].

In the Six-Day War, nearly a quarter-million Palestinians from the West Bank moved to Jordan, many by force. It wasn't easy for them to return, and not all managed to do so. This is where the danger lies when the possibility of transfer becomes part of the political discourse, when it seemingly becomes a legitimate subject. Like military orders that have a black flag hanging over their illegality, there are ideas that should have black flags over them.

Ephraim Sneh doesn't usually think in moral-humanistic terms.

Like a good Mapainik, he thinks about what's feasible.* If he could take a few minutes off from plotting his transfer plans, he should go over to the government secretariat's office and look up the minutes of the meeting from July 21, 1948. He'll find the following comments by then-agriculture minister Aharon Tzizling, who believed that expulsion was not only immoral, but it also threatened the security of the fledgling state. "There are still those who are not properly assessing what kind of enemy is growing outside the borders of our state. Our enemies from the Arab states are nothing compared to those hundreds of thousands who, out of hatred, frustration, and bottomless enmity, will storm our state, no matter what kind of arrangement is made," said the minister. He meant the refugees, many of whom are still in camps and with them second-, third- and even fourth-generation refugees, some of whom have become suicide bombers. It's doubtful that there are many other predictions that were proven to be as accurate, and as tragic, as his.

April 5, 2002

---

* Mapai, the forerunner to today's Labor Party, represented the Zionist mainstream and controlled the Israeli government until 1977.

37

THE TURNING POINT

Meron Benvenisti

NO ONE HAS ever been able to predict exactly when the opposition to war and bloodshed turns from treachery into a legitimate, indeed proper approach; when moral condemnation of acts of war becomes politically correct—and when a phrase like "a war for our homes" changes from being a battle cry into blathering nonsense. Nobody has predicted it in advance, but experience shows that the moment when the patriotism of the herd turns into critical skepticism does inevitably arrive, sooner or later—sometimes in weeks or months, or sometimes a generation or two later.

Past experience proves that international condemnations, exposure to the horror, demonstrations and political protests have a cumulative influence, but those are countered by feelings of tribal unity, moral superiority and self-righteousness. One would expect that the price of the bloodshed from the continuing violence would lead to a rational calculation of the value of human lives versus the goals for which they are killed. But communities that grow used to calculating their steps according to absolute values do not do so according to pragmatic assessments of cost and benefit. Even making the comparison between the cost in human lives and its purpose is problematic: The most costly price has already been paid in human lives, and the need to justify it requires inflating the value of what they were paid for.

Leaders who inflict great sacrifices upon their people cannot let it be known to all and sundry that they were wrong, so they make the goals absolute: "A war for our homes" or "a war for our existence"—goals with infinite price tags. The issue of the relationship between the goal to its price is decried as irrelevant, and raising rational arguments is considered blasphemy, an attempt to quantify something that has no price.

Nonetheless, experience shows that manipulating values to justify the sacrifice of human lives can never succeed because the survival instinct is stronger than the manipulation. Eventually, the cynicism of inflated, counterfeit patriotism is revealed, as happened in the Lebanon war.

Nobody can predict when the moment will come and all the experts and commentators will start competing over who was the first to expose the failure, the misguided strategy, the uselessness, the illusions, the political stupidity, the surrender to vengeance and the ruthlessness—the real price of the current operation. But the manipulators should not delude themselves: That moment will come. Will it arrive when the scenes of destruction in Jenin are finally revealed? Or when it becomes clear to everyone that the operation "to eliminate the terrorist infrastructure" only increased the terror? Or when it turns out that the reoccupation of the Palestinian territories and the buffer zones requires longer and longer reserve service? Will the sobering-up occur when Israel becomes a "rogue state" in the eyes of the entire world, or will it happen when the economic situation deteriorates into an even worse crisis?

And if anyone has doubts about the arrival of the morning after, they should take a look at the Jewish Agency's patriotic advertising campaign, which calls on people to "continue living the dream"—a pathetic attempt to postpone the awakening on the shards of the Zionist dream and to preach getting lost in dreams to escape reality.

When the time comes, and the curtain is pulled away from this phony patriotism, it will turn out that the fifth Israel-Palestine war (after the 1936–39 Arab Revolt, the 1948 war, the Lebanon war, and the first intifada) will truly have been another battle in the war of independence—not Israel's, as Ariel Sharon claims, but that of the Palestinians. And nobody, neither side, will win that war, because in conflicts between communities there are no victors, only losers. All that will remain will be the horrific memories, the profound hatred, the calls for vengeance, and the bitter taste of missed opportunities, since it almost, almost could have been different.

April 11, 2002

CONTRIBUTORS

SHULAMIT ALONI, who founded Israel's Civil Rights Movement in 1973, has worked as a journalist and teacher and was a Member of the Knesset from 1974 to 1996. She was Minister of Communications and the Arts, Science and Technology for the Meretz Party from 1992 to 1996.

URI AVNERY, who was born in Germany and fought in the 1948 war, was publisher and editorial writer of the magazine *Haolam Hazeh* from 1950 to 1990 and has served in the Knesset. In 1992 he helped found Gush Shalom, the Peace Bloc, which advocates an end to Israel's occupation and the creation of a Palestinian state, with Jerusalem recognized as the joint capital of Israel and Palestine.

AMI AYALON served under both Labor and Likud governments as the head of Israel's General Security Service (Shabak, or Shin Bet) from February 1996 to May 2000.

MICHAEL BEN-YAIR was an acting justice on the Supreme Court for six months in 1990. From 1993 to 1996 he served as Israel's Attorney General under Yitzhak Rabin, Shimon Peres, and Benjamin Netanyahu.

MERON BENVENISTI, a former Deputy Mayor of Jerusalem and a frequent contributor to *Ha'aretz*, is the author of several books, including *Intimate Enemies: Jews and Arabs in a Shared Land* and *Sacred Landscape: The Buried History of the Holy Land Since 1948*.

YIGAL BRONNER teaches Sanskrit and South Asian studies at Tel Aviv University and is an activist in Ta'ayush, the Arab-Jewish Partnership.

NETA GOLAN is with the International Solidarity Movement, which places international civilians in the occupied territories for the sake of non-violent resistance against the occupation. She was among the 40 international observers who joined Yasser Arafat's in his besieged Ramallah compound in April 2002. Ian Urbina is associate editor of the Washington-based magazine *Middle East Report*.

NEVE GORDON is the former director of Physicians for Human Rights, Israel, and currently teaches politics at Ben-Gurion University in Beer-Sheva. He is currently active in Ta'ayush.

DAVID GROSSMAN is the author of five novels as well as two works of journalism, *The Yellow Wind* and *Sleeping on a Wire: Conversations with Palestinians in Israel*.

JEFF HALPER is a professor of anthropology and the coordinator of the Israeli Committee Against House Demolitions.

AMIRA HASS, who covers Palestinian affairs for *Ha'aretz*, is the author of *Drinking the Sea at Gaza: Days and Nights in a Land Under Siege*.

A professor of sociology at Hebrew University in Jerusalem, BARUCH KIMMERLING's works include *The Interrupted System: Israeli Civilians in War and Routine Times, Palestinians: The Making of a People* (with Joel Migdal) and, most recently, *The Invention and Decline of Israeliness: State, Society, and the Military*.

YITZHAK LAOR is the author of six books of poetry and three novels. In 1972 he served a prison term for refusal to serve in the territories, and in 1985, the government banned his play *Ephraim Goes Back to the Army,* though the ruling was later overturned by Israel's Supreme Court. He teaches at Tel Aviv University.

AVIV LAVIE reports on the media for *Ha'aretz.*

SHAMAI LEIBOWITZ, a graduate of Yeshivat Har Etzion, is an attorney in Tel Aviv.

ANTHONY LEWIS is a two-time Pulitzer Prize winner. He was a columnist for the *New York Times* from 1969 to 2001 and is James Madison Visiting Professor at Columbia University.

GIDEON LEVY writes the weekly "Twilight Zone" column for *Ha'aretz.*

ISHAI MENUCHIN is a major in the Israel Defense Forces reserves and chairman of Yesh Gvul, the soldiers' movement for selective refusal.

ADI OPHIR is a professor of philosophy at the Cohn Institute of History and Philosophy of Science at Tel Aviv University. Among his most recent publications is *The Order of Evils: Toward an Ontology of Morals,* a treatise in moral philosophy.

ASSAF ORON, a sergeant major in the Giv'ati Brigade, was one of the original 53 signers of the January 2002 reserve officers' letter of refusal.

ILAN PAPPÉ is a senior lecturer in political science at Haifa University and the academic director of the Research Institute for Peace at Givat Haviva. His recent books include *The Making of the Arab-Israeli Conflict, 1948–1951* and *The Israel/Palestine Question.*

TANYA REINHART is a professor of linguistics at Tel Aviv University. Her political columns have appeared since 1994 in *Yediot Ahronot* and on ZNet. She is the author of *Israel/Palestine: How to End the War of 1948.*

TOM SEGEV is the author of *The Seventh Million; One Palestine, Complete;* and *Elvis in Jerusalem,* and a columnist for *Ha'aretz.*

AVI SHLAIM is a professor of international relations at St. Antony's College, Oxford University. His books include *Collusion Across the Jordan, War and Peace in the Middle East,* and *The Iron Wall: Israel and the Arab World.*

DR. YIGAL SHOCHAT served as a fighter pilot in the Israeli Air Force and was shot down over Egypt in 1970 during the War of Attrition, losing his right leg. He went on to become Surgeon General of the Air Force and is now a volunteer with Physicians for Human Rights.

ZE'EV STERNHELL, who teaches political science at Hebrew University in Jerusalem, is the author of *Neither Right Nor Left, The Birth of Fascist Ideology,* and *The Founding Myths of Israel.*

GILA SVIRSKY has served as director of the New Israel Fund and of Bat Shalom (the Israeli side of The Jerusalem Link: A Women's Joint Venture for Peace) and as chair of B'Tselem, the Israeli Information Center for Human Rights in the Occupied Territories. After the beginning of the second intifada, she co-founded and coordinates the Coalition of Women for a Just Peace.

SERGIO YAHNI is co-director of the Alternative Information Center, Israel/Palestine. Since 1989 he has been sentenced to jail three times for refusing to serve in the occupied territories. Following the eruption of the second intifada he has refused to serve in Israel's military in any capacity, and was therefore sentenced to 28 days in prison.